C000065134

Contents

ALL THE QUEEN'S HORSES
A Golden Jubilee Tribute to Her Majesty The Queen

Front cover image by gracious permission of Her Majesty the Queen. Photography by Henry Dallal

Published by MDA Publishing Ltd, Southbank House, Black Prince Road, London, SE1 7SJ
Tel 020 7463 2020
Fax 020 7793 4059
Email: info@mdacomms.com

Printed on Nimrod Silk 150gsm
Paper Supplied by Gerald Judd Sales Ltd. Printed by Stephens&George

Images kindly supplied by the following: Camerapress, Central Press, Hulton Getty, Independent Picture Library, National Pictures, Only Horses Picture Agency, PA Photo, The Royal Collection, The Scotsman.

Editor: Michael Dewar
Authors: Michael Clayton, Sir Michael Oswald, Michael Dewar
Design: James Dewar, Jeremy Owen, James Greenfield, Lisa Crowe, Piers Milburn

Advertising Executives:
James Lyall Grant, Robert Hodgson, Joe Paterson, Martin McMormack
Tel: 020 7463 2244
Fax: 020 7793 4059
jameslg@mdacomms.com

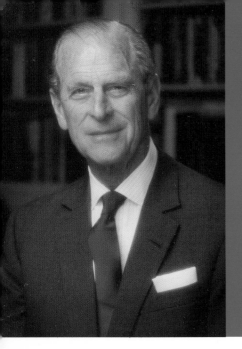

Foreword by
HRH The Duke of Edinburgh

'All the Queen's Horses' is a very special tribute to the Queen in her Golden Jubilee Year from the equestrian community. We all know what a special interest and support the Queen has shown to virtually every aspect of the partnership between people and horses.

It might be assumed that interest in horses would have declined in this mechanical age, but I am quite sure that this all-embracing display will demonstrate that this partnership is as strong, if not stronger, than ever.

'All the Queen's Horses' is a major undertaking and I would like to take this opportunity to thank everyone taking part for their contribution to this very special event.

The

John Lewis Partnership

congratulates

Her Majesty The Queen

on her

Golden Jubilee.

WAITROSE   John Lewis

All the Queens Horses

In 1997 the much-heralded Pageant of the Horse, which was to celebrate the Golden Wedding Anniversary of The Queen and Prince Philip in the Great Park, Windsor disappeared in a mud bath. The worst July weather for nearly a century dashed the hopes of the Committee and Production Team who had been preparing for the event for two years and the 1,000 participants who had been rehearsing for many months.

A telephone call to the Mother of an eight year old taking part with the Pony Club summed up the feelings of many: "How am I going to tell my daughter, who has not slept for the past week with excitement, that it is cancelled".

Undeterred, Colonel Sir Piers Bengough the Pageant's Chairman, called the Committee together to discuss the future. It was determined that it was worth continuing to plan for the next event and the focus of this would be The Queen's Golden Jubilee. Although five years away it was quite clear that the equestrian world meant and wanted to pay Tribute to their Sovereign for the support and interest Her Majesty had shown in the horse world.

For the next three years the project bubbled gently away until the Millennium Celebrations brought the Committee back together again to decide on the next stage. Although the content was important, what was vital to the preparations was the venue. The Committee felt it too risky to put the event back into the Great Park and the hunt was on for an alternative. Hyde Park and Horse Guards – after the success of the Royal Military Tattoo – were studied in depth but discarded on grounds of cost, restrictions and dates.

The answer came from those close to The Queen. Why not hold it at the horse show where The Queen's involvement and interest has spanned the past 60 years – The Royal Windsor Horse Show. Set beneath the magnificent Windsor Castle, surely this was the ideal venue. The horse show organisers were asked and the project had a home and a host.

Next came the title. 'All The Queen's Horses' seemed to sum up the story that we were trying to convey. Although the Golden Jubilee plans are to have a multitude of public celebrations, All The Queen's Horses has been specifically produced to reflect a very private interest.

Although the concept of 1,000 horses and music from the Pageant continued to provide the enduring theme for 'All The Queen's Horses', it was decided to cover the sixty years of Royal Windsor and The Queen's 50 years since Her Accession to the Throne. Unfinished business the Pageant might be but a fresh look, a new script and a more contemporary musical score was required to ensure that the event provided a real Tribute to our Sovereign.

The next step was to make it a National and International celebration. Participants as far away as Kenya, Pakistan, India and Canada were recruited and the BBC gave their commitment to broadcasting the largest equestrian 'spectacular' ever staged.

And what a stage! A forty-foot high Lion and Unicorn 'proscenium' arch surrounding a stage for a 150 voice choir and a 75 piece Orchestra is the central feature below Windsor Castle. The 130m x 60m arena has a weatherproof covering to ensure

that the vagaries of the May weather are not allowed to spoil the occasion.

Star names, such as Anthony Andrews, Dame Judi Dench, Sir Derek Jacobi, Robert Hardy, Prunella Scales and Edward Woodward, were signed up, dancers were employed and military and civilian musicians merged together to produce a unique score.

The build of the event required a new electrical sub station, miles of steel work, huge lighting towers to support over 1,000 stage lights and sound system worthy of a rock concert. There has been an army of crew working all hours and in all weather to produce the design that has been subject to continual tinkering since the start of the project.

It has been a massive but worthwhile project. It is hoped that not only do we produce a Tribute that says "Thank you, Your Majesty" but also contributes to Equine Charities.

Finally, although it is inappropriate to thank specific people on such a large and time consuming project - particularly as there is an army of professionals and volunteers involved with running the show - there are a few that have lived and breathed the event for the past two years and without whom this spectacular event would not have got past first base. These include; the ever-imaginative Producer Major Sir Michael Parker, the Project Director Mike Shephard, the Commercial Director Nigel Rushman and the supportive Crown Equerry Lieutenant Colonel Seymour Gilbart-Denham.

Lastly, a special thanks from everybody should go to Colonel Sir Piers Bengough, the inspirational Chairman who with boundless energy and buckets of good humour, has always led from the front, mostly at the charge.

Simon Brooks-Ward
Director, All The Queen's Horses

These exclusive pictures of HM The Queen taken recently especially for All The Queen's Horses show the Queen with Tinkerbell (right), the mother of both Peter Pan (centre) and the year old foal Tiger Lily (left)

All three horses are homebred at the Royal Mews and are what is known as skewbald in their colouring

50 Glorious Years

The Coronation of Queen Elizabeth in June 1953 was almost certainly the most magnificent and influential royal ceremony of the twentieth century. The Coronation provided the opportunity to display a new kind of imperial greatness by linking together the Commonwealth and the British Empire for which two World Wars had been fought. The British people made the Coronation a day of rejoicing and pride in their country and, for the first time ever, the entire nation was involved – thanks to the arrival of television. Celebrations began ten days before the Coronation when a million people invaded the capital to see the decorations and walk the royal route. The nation's newspapers were, seemingly, full of nothing but the forthcoming event, feeding the dramatic surge of interest and the gathering euphoria.

The Royal garden party on May 29 was like a Hollywood extravaganza, the royal stars supported by a phalanx of extras including generals, admirals, bishops, sultans, sheiks and African tribesmen. The women guests were beautifully dressed in silks, taffetas and gros-grain and Elizabeth seemed animated and happy as she walked from one group to another.

A magnificent dinner and ball was held by the Household Brigade at Hampton Court and Prime Minister Winston Churchill held a lunch at Buckingham Palace for all the Commonwealth leaders who had come from the four corners of the world.

The young Elizabeth appeared to thoroughly enjoy all the many proceedings, smiling happily, looking confident and remarkably relaxed. Despite her Coronation being the most important single event of her young life Elizabeth still had time for other matters.

Days before the great event, a lady-in-waiting commented, 'You must be feeling nervous Ma'am'. Elizabeth replied, 'Of course I am, but I really do think Aureole will win', referring to one of her favourite horses running that week in the Derby. Coronation Day – June 2, 1953 – was remarkable mainly for the size and exuberance of the crowds despite the unseasonal cold and wet weather. And Elizabeth enchanted the cheering crowds. Photographer and designer, Cecil Beaton described Elizabeth thus:

'The cheeks are sugar-pink: her hair tightly curled around the Victorian diadem of precious stones straight on her brow. Her pink hands are folded meekly on the elaborate grandeur of her encrusted skirt; she is still a young girl with a demeanour of simplicity and humility. Perhaps her mother has taught her never to use a superfluous gesture. As she walks she allows her heavy skirt to swing backwards and forwards in a beautiful rhythmic effect. This girlish figure has enormous dignity; she belongs in this scene of almost Byzantine magnificence.'

The Coronation service began with the Archbishop of Canterbury's declaration to the bishops in the sanctuary. 'Sirs, I here present unto you Queen Elizabeth, your undoubted Queen.' And the culmination of the proceedings was the moment the Archbishop of Canterbury placed the heavy crown on Elizabeth's head. This was immediately followed by the roaring acclamation from all those crowded into Westminster Abbey, 'God Save Queen Elizabeth. Long Live Queen Elizabeth, May the Queen live for Ever.'

The young Queen Elizabeth then rose slowly to her feet and walked back down the aisle out into the cool, wet day to the Coronation coach which was

The Queen in the Coronation coach, June 1953

Queen Elizabeth II
is the 40th monarch
since William the
Conqueror obtained
the crown of England

Top: The Queen at Her
Coronation ceremony in
Westminster Abbey in
June 1953. Her mother
looks on from above

drawn by eight magnificent greys. With the heavy crown on her head and holding the Sceptre and Orb, the Queen was escorted to Buckingham Palace by thirteen thousand troops, twenty-nine bands and twenty-seven carriages. It was a magnificent and powerful spectacle for throughout the journey a great thunder of acclamation heralded and pursued the procession as the newly-crowned Queen was taken along the seven mile route to the palace. It was a remarkable occasion and one that Elizabeth enjoyed and in which the whole nation revelled.

For the first few years of her reign, Elizabeth was the subject of adulation throughout the land. She became the beacon of hope and expectation for a new Elizabethan age. As Jock Colville, private secretary to Winston Churchill and later Princess Elizabeth commented, 'Never has a monarch received such adulation.' And Princess Margaret read the mood of the nation when she commented, "The Coronation was like a phoenix-time. Everything was being raised from the ashes. There was this gorgeous-looking, lovely young lady, and nothing to stop anything getting better and better." Britain was getting back on its feet and the post-war recovery was advancing apace. There was a dramatic upsurge in the nation's birth rate - a

natural aftermath after such a long, hard, titanic struggle in which, for the first time, both civilians as well as members of the armed forces had been targeted and bombed by an enemy. But the feeling of euphoria sweeping Britain would not last. The harsh realities of imperial decline, foreign competition and the advance of communism were becoming increasingly evident.

Six months after the Coronation, the Queen and Prince Philip embarked on a historic Commonwealth tour which lasted a remarkable five and a half months, the longest marathon ever undertaken by a British Head of State. Together, they visited Bermuda, Jamaica, Fiji, Tonga, the Coco Islands, Aden, Uganda, Malta and Gibraltar but the majority of the tour was spent in Australia and New Zealand. Millions of people turned out to see and fete the young Queen and her handsome husband. It was indeed a huge success but the tour would become the pinnacle of the Windsor Monarchy's world-wide prestige in the twentieth century.

In future, the numbers who would turn out to see and cheer the Queen during such tours were never so great because the advent of television made it unnecessary for people to line the streets or assemble in a great stadium in order to see their Queen. On a personal level, of course, Elizabeth's entire life has been remarkable. The teenage princess earned the admiration and respect of the nation during World War 11 when she donned army uniform and joined the ATS (Auxiliary Territorial Service) as a Subaltern, training as a driver and mechanic. This was no photo opportunity or publicity stunt for Elizabeth insisted on completing the course that every other ATS girl undertook. She took the driving and mechanical examinations and passed both. In 1947, the International Artists' Committee in New York voted her one of the most glamorous women in the world. Two months later, Time magazine declared her 'the Woman of the Week' and noted her 'Pin-Up' charm.

In the first three years of her marriage Elizabeth gave birth to a son and heir, Prince Charles in 1948, followed by Princess Anne in 1950. Ten years later Andrew arrived and finally Edward in 1964; a remarkable family for a working monarch. Throughout her life, Elizabeth has been supported by the energetic, forceful and restless Prince Philip who has proved a tower of strength. As a constitutional monarch who is above party politics, the Queen has on many occasions proved an invaluable asset in forging closer links with other nations. It is difficult to exaggerate the respect which the Queen has earned for Britain as a direct result of her quiet, educated, sophisticated professionalism. Throughout her reign the Queen has hosted countless lunches and dinners at

Top left: Princess Elizabeth and Prince Philip on honeymoon at Broadlands

Top centre: The late Queen Mother and the Queen on the way to Ascot

Top right: The Gold Coronation Coach carries the Queen from Westminster Abbey

Left: Her Majesty The Queen on her way to the State Opening of Parliament

Buckingham Palace for Heads of Government from around the globe; attended official functions, grand evenings, lunches, dinners, cocktail parties and informal gatherings in foreign countries during innumerable royal visits. Throughout her long reign she has shown a remarkable dedication, aptitude and deftness of touch on every private and public occasion. The epitome of discretion and diplomacy, the Queen has helped to enhance world leaders' opinions of Britain and the nation.

Much good would flow from the designation of the Queen as 'Head of the Commonwealth' a position which the Queen has been most proud to hold. Indeed, the Queen has seen the Commonwealth as her special sphere of

interest and, as a result, has given the Palace a Commonwealth perspective separate from that of British governments. Her friendships and familiarity with Commonwealth political leaders throughout the last fifty years has provided a valuable continuity which has helped the Commonwealth family survive and flourish.

The Queen has always regarded her role as Head of the Commonwealth and as Head of State of her various realms with a seriousness that has never diminished despite Britain's closer ties with Europe. That interest was forged when her father, King George V1, was on the throne for he attached great importance to the Empire. In 1947, Elizabeth vowed, 'My whole life, whether it be long or short, will be

Above: The Queen has always gone for strong colours in her choice of dress

Right: The Queen and President Ronald Reagan ride out together in Winsdor Great Park

devoted to the service of our great Imperial family to which we all belong'. The Queen has visited every Commonwealth country and has always been warmly welcomed by crowds of well-wishers. She has not simply been a symbol but, more importantly, an active force. It has been said that, whereas she inherited the title of Queen of England, her Headship of the Commonwealth is something she has striven for and earned. Sir Sonny Ramphal, who became the Secretariat's longest serving and most influential Secretary-General, regarded the Queen's role as crucial, saying, 'The Queen brought an understanding that it was a post-colonial Commonwealth... She brought a quality of caring, a sense that it was an important dimension of her reign... She grew up with the new, young Commonwealth leaders, understood them and related to them'.

As a result, the Queen has earned the personal loyalty of Commonwealth leaders, an extraordinary achievement in view of the ideological differences of many of them. Over the highly contentious issue of Rhodesia, when many Commonwealth leaders looked on Britain with distrust, there was a real possibility of the Commonwealth breaking up. Some diplomats closely involved with the critical Lusaka Accord maintain that it was the Queen 'who managed to hold the whole thing together'. It was a remarkable achievement for many African leaders at that Lusaka conference were prepared to walk out but stayed and signed the Accord out of loyalty,

Left and above: The Queen has always accorded great importance to Commonwealth occasions

respect and admiration for the Queen. That settlement led eight months later to an ending of war in Rhodesia, the restoration of legality and the launching of the new independent state of Zimbabwe.

Throughout the last fifty years there has been an understandable move by many Commonwealth nations to become politically independent of Britain and there was a fear that the Commonwealth might simply become a tenuous association of like-minded third world countries. But the Commonwealth flourished and this was largely due to the strong attachment between these states and Buckingham Palace. These Commonwealth leaders recognised that in Queen Elizabeth they had a sovereign whom they trusted no matter how closely linked Britain became to Europe. To many Commonwealth citizens the Queen was seen as a person with interests and emotions not a constitutional piece of machinery. As Lord Charteris, who worked with the Queen for twenty-seven years, and attended many of her confidential talks with Commonwealth leaders, commented, 'They tell her all their troubles and worries; she's like a mother confessor.' For her part, the Queen has been equally determined to ensure that the Commonwealth would not simply

wither on the vine. In the past thirty years there have been a number of senior politicians who have been under the misapprehension that the Commonwealth was about to die but most accept that one of the reasons it has not done so is because at its head is the Queen. Like her father and grand-father before her, the Queen believes fervently in the Commonwealth as a family of nations and she is determined that this will continue.

At home, one of the principal duties of the Queen is leading the nation at times of grief and sorrow. Each and every November she is seen by the entire nation, a diminutive figure dressed in black, laying a wreath at the Cenotaph in Whitehall in memory of those who gave their lives in two World Wars. All comment how the Queen strikes the right note on such occasions, particularly those who meet the Queen in such circumstances when they have suffered the pain of a loss or serious injury.

The horrific Aberfan disaster in October 1966, when a pit-heap collapsed in South Wales engulfing a school and killing one hundred and forty-six people, was a prime example of the Queen's empathy with grieving communities. She went to

Aberfan and walked through the stricken area, meeting and talking to grieving parents whose children had died. It was also one of the few occasions when the Queen was so overcome with emotion that tears flowed as she talked to a group of women who had lost their children. As a result, the women of Aberfan have for ever loved the Queen for her warmth, her understanding and her tears of compassion.

Throughout Queen Elizabeth's reign Britain has found itself involved in a number of wars. Of course, the Queen – more than most of her subjects – has a close experience of war. She was a teenage girl living in London throughout the blitz. She witnessed the nightly bombing raids; she saw devastation at first hand; she watched the anguish on peoples' faces and, on occasions, she saw the wounded and the dying.

The 1960s found the Queen at the centre of the Rhodesian crisis when both Prime Minister Harold Wilson and the Rhodesian Prime Minister Ian Smith 'claimed' the Monarch in their legal arguments. The Rhodesian government tried to distinguish between their beloved Sovereign and Harold Wilson. For his part, the British Prime Minister wanted to detach the Rhodesian people from a rebellious government. Even after Ian Smith declared UDI both sides continued to 'claim' the Queen in their political feud. Ian Smith went to extraordinary lengths to maintain the fiction that Rhodesia, though independent, was a Monarchy but in 1970 it did become a republic. It would be a further ten years before the country returned to the Commonwealth, partly due to the Queen's behind-the-scenes encouragement. In 1973, the Monarchy was embroiled in another constitutional crisis, high-lighting the anomaly of the royal prerogative in countries of which the Queen remained Head of State, when the Governor-General of Australia sacked the Prime Minister, Gough Whitlam.

In Britain, the 'seventies' saw an escalation of sectarian violence in Northern Ireland, and hyper-inflation, nation-wide strikes and serious economic problems. The Queen, however, remained the image of stability in this turbulent world, portraying a measured calm based on the well-established, long-lasting image of the royal family with its emphasis on the family.

But, despite the fragile political and economic climate it was decided that the Jubilee celebrations should go ahead and the Queen not only toured Britain but also visited all the countries of the world of which she was the monarch. The celebrations, which some had feared might become a damp squib, became a roaring success, due mainly to the enthusiasm, the charm and the joy the Queen exuded during her many walkabouts and informal chats with everyone she met. Literally millions of people turned out to see and cheer the Queen that year. A million people turned out on one day to cheer her as she rode with Prince Philip from the Palace for a special service at St. Paul's Cathedral. And tens of millions of people up-and-down the country enjoyed informal street parties. There was a genuine feeling that both the Queen and her cheering subjects were enjoying the occasion together and there was a natural personal respect and affection for the Queen. As Lord Charteris commented, 'She had a love affair with the country'.

Newspapers and magazines were full of profiles

analysing her life and her interests. They noted that the Queen was passionately involved in horses and horse-racing, dogs and field sports. On a personal level, she enjoyed riding, walking and stalking. And yet, the profiles recorded that the Queen also enjoyed more ordinary pleasures like scrabble, jigsaw puzzles and watching comedies on tv. It was noted the Queen ate and drank little and did not smoke but that she did enjoy chatting with staff at her various homes and listening to gossip below stairs. Sir John Colville commented, 'She has reigned for twenty-five years without putting a foot wrong. She has the qualities of patience, courtesy, a sense of dignity, judgement, self-control and wisdom.'

In 1982, however, the Queen once again found herself closely involved in a war situation – the Falklands War. She was the monarch of the country whose sovereignty had been invaded; Head of the Commonwealth which included the Falklands; Head of the British forces despatched to recapture them and, also, the mother of a serving Royal Naval officer. The Queen let it be known that she would not, for one minute, countenance the idea of Prince Andrew being exempted from active service because of his royal status. More recently, large numbers of British troops were involved in the Gulf War after Iraq's invasion of Kuwait, and many battalions have served as peace-keepers in Bosnia and Kosovo following the break-up of the former Yugoslavia.

During her reign, the Queen has also been called upon to show personal bravery when faced with danger. In June 1981, the Queen was riding down the Mall at the head of the Household Cavalry for the annual Trooping the Colour when six single shots rang out and her black Canadian

mare, Burmese, was startled and reared up. The Queen remained almost still, calming Burmese, as members of the Household Cavalry, who had been trained for such an eventuality, cantered forward to protect her and cut off any assailant. Prince Charles and the Prince Philip, riding a couple of yards behind the Queen, instantly spurred their horses forward to shield her. The incident was over in a moment or so but coming less than two years after the murder of Lord Mountbatten it was an alarming incident. The Queen handled the situation calmly and with the minimum of fuss. The Daily Express declared, 'In every pub and club throughout the land the verdict is the same. Her Majesty showed guts, courage, pluck, bravery and bottle.'

Twelve months later the Queen would face a sterner and more personal test to her courage when she awoke suddenly one morning to find a strange man standing by her bedside with a blood-stained broken ashtray in his hand. But she did not scream nor call for help. She remained calm and discreetly pressed the alarm button by the side of her bed as she held the man in conversation. It took two panic calls and more than fifteen minutes before anyone responded. Fortunately, the young man – Michael Fagan – made no attempt to attack the Queen. But this lapse of security had coincided with an IRA campaign of violence on the mainland.

The marriage of Prince Charles to Lady Diana Spencer touched millions of people not only in Britain but across the world. Their glorious wedding, which was seen live by satellite throughout the industrialised world, heralded an upsurge of admiration and affection for the Royal family. Prince Charles was admired as the 'consummate prince'

Left: Princess Elizabeth joined the ATS in 1945

Right: The young princess with a working horse

Far left: Her Royal Majesty talks to some of the Chelsea Pensioners at the Royal Hospital's Founder's Day Parade in Summer 1962

Above: The moment when blank shots were fired from a starting pistol in the mall

Opposite page: Her Majesty The Queen Elizabeth on Burmese, whom she rode for many years at the annual Trooping of The Colour

and Diana as the 'flawless, beautiful, shy princess'. As the world is only too well aware, the 1990s was the decade of royal marriage breakdowns with three of the Queen's children - Princess Anne Prince Charles and the Duke of York - separating and divorcing in turn. And then there were pictures of a 'shocked and devastated Queen standing under the walls of Windsor Castle as the fire tore the heart out of her favourite home. Four days later she made her famous 'annus horribilis' speech. It was moving, open and spoken from the heart.

Whatever politicians and newspaper editorials say of the Queen she takes comfort in the ever-increasing size of her mailbag. The letter writers are usually ordinary people expressing concern, wishing her well and offering their support. The Queen appears tireless, carrying out more engagements than twenty years ago. She also shows no lack of enthusiasm for the job. To see her visiting a hospital, talking to school children or on a walkabout, is to witness a woman who still enjoys meeting and chatting to people from all walks of life. And she always enjoys a laugh.

The Queen has been fortunate in those she has gathered around her and who have supported her in a world that has changed dramatically during her fifty years on the throne. Though surrounded by courtiers, advisers and officials, in reality the Queen

has principally relied on a small nucleus of close confidants and good friends, as well as the highly intelligent Prince Philip, who have provided the necessary strength, courage and advice.

Above all, of course, has been the Queen's remarkably close life-long relationship with her beloved mother, a strong, ambitious, down-to-earth, charismatic and loving figure. Without a doubt the Queen Mother has been both a guiding light and a rock of stability to her daughter who has helped her become the monarch so admired and respected by all. There have been others but none so close as the Queen Mother. Throughout the reign virtually never a day has passed without the two women talking to each other, at least by phone. Their relationship changed over time from that of mother and daughter to two committed women with great love and admiration for each other and an implacable trust. With her death in March 2002 the Queen has suffered a grievous loss.

Outside her immediate family, there have been other people with whom the Queen has forged strong friendships but they are few in number though they have been hugely important to her. For many years 'Bobo' MacDonald, her Scottish nursemaid who became her mentor, was a woman of formidable authority in whom the Queen confided on a daily basis over a myriad of subjects

The fire during Winsdor Castle in 1992 - the Queen's annus horribilis

and over many decades. The Queen respected Bobo's strong Scottish principles, her down-to-earth views and her understanding of the common man.

The late Harry Porchester, whom the Queen affectionately nicknamed 'Porchey', first met Elizabeth after the war when they sang madrigals together at Buckingham Palace each week. Elizabeth and 'Porchey' - later Lord Carnarvon – shared a growing interest in horses and riding and the two were destined to have a close lifelong friendship. 'Porchey' became someone who was very important to the Queen, a close personal friend as well as her Racing Manager.

And, of course, there was 'Uncle Dickie' - Lord Mountbatten – Prince Philip's uncle who was a great source of advice, good counsel and plain speaking during the early years of Elizabeth's reign. Uncle Dickie was someone to whom Elizabeth could turn for advice other than her senior courtiers. To Philip, Uncle Dickie had been surrogate father, friend, mentor and benefactor and advised Philip in the courting of the teenage Elizabeth. Mountbatten had also been a loyal and wise supporter of the monarchy. His assassination by the IRA in August 1979 was a cruel blow to the Royal Family and especially to Prince Charles who looked upon him as a father figure.

During the past forty years, Lady Susan Hussey – now the Queen's principal Lady-in-Waiting - has become one of her most influential advisers and also a close friend. The two spend time each day discussing future commitments and arrangements.

Throughout her reign, the Queen has been able to rely on the sound advice and honest counsel of her most senior courtiers, all highly intelligent, honourable and meticulous administrators. After the first eighteen months of her reign Sir Alan Lascelles, adviser to four monarchs, was succeeded by Michael Adeane, an hereditary courtier with a wry sense of humour who was devoted to the Queen.

In 1972 Sir Martin Charteris, the Queen's assistant private secretary, stepped into Adeane's shoes, marking the end of a long era of 'hereditary' private secretaries going back to the 1930s. His arrival brought a change of style to the palace and the Queen encouraged his more youthful, up-beat, colourful vision of the monarchy. In 1977, Sir Philip Moore, was handed the top job. Twelve years later, Sir Robert Fellowes, the brother-in-law of Lady Diana Spencer, took over the reins. In 2002 Her Majesty Queen Elizabeth II remains as popular as ever. Through the ups and downs of 50 years of history she has remained a constant, a rock to the British people and to the Commonwealth.

BY APPOINTMENT TO H.R.H. THE PRINCE OF WALES
PURVEYORS OF CHAMPAGNE - CHAMPAGNE LAURENT-PERRIER
CHAMPAGNE
ESTD 1812
Laurent-Perrier
BRUT L.P.

Jaeger-LeCoultre

The Jaeger-LeCoultre story begins nearly 170 years ago in the Vallée de Joux, high in the Jura mountains above Geneva. Huguenots fleeing religious persecution had settled in the small farming community of Le Sentier in the 16th century, and it was two descendants of these famous skilled Protestant craftsmen, Antoine LeCoultre and his brother Ulysse, who established a watchmaking workshop in the village in 1833.

The winters in the Jura are harsh and long, and between October and May farmers would find themselves cut off from the outside world. Many were imbued with the Huguenot passion for precision engineering and spent the long winter months producing mechanical devices. But even in a community renowned for its technical ingenuity, Antoine LeCoultre stood out as an innovative genius. It was LeCoultre, for instance, who established the metric system as the watch industry's measurement standard when, in 1844, he invented his Millionometer, the first instrument capable of measuring components to the nearest millionth of a meter.

In 1903 the partnership of Jaeger-LeCoultre was born when Antoine's grandson, Jacques-David LeCoultre, joined forces with the Paris chronometer-maker Edmond Jaeger and so inaugurated the era in which the company developed the three classic lines for which it is celebrated by horological connoisseurs the world over today.

First, in 1928, came the Atmos, the magical mantel clock that lives on air. So impressed with the design was the Swiss Confederation that it adopted it as a favourite gift for visiting statesmen: the homes of Winston Churchill and John F. Kennedy both displayed the clock prominently.

In 1931 there followed one of the authentic design masterpieces of the Art Deco era, the Reverso. Where the Atmos, which was powered by tiny changes in air temperature, had been produced in response to the demand for a mechanism that did not need to be wound up, the Reverso was developed to meet an altogether different kind of practical challenge. British Army officers in India were frustrated to discover that existing wristwatches were simply not hardy enough to withstand the knocks they habitually received on the polo field. They therefore approached Jaeger-LeCoultre to create a watch chic enough to suit their status but sufficiently tough to survive the rough and tumble of the sporting life. It was thus that design engineer René-Alfred Chauvot conceived the idea of the rectangular swivel case that remains the unmistakable identifying feature of the Reverso to this day.

Then, twenty years later, the third enduring Jaeger-LeCoultre design classic, the round-faced Memovox, made its first appearance on the market.

All three of these classic and unique lines are set to continue to blaze a bright trail of innovation into the 21st century. For instance, this year sees the launch of the Reverso Septantième. Increasing the size of its case still further ensures an extreme level of technical performance with its functions now guaranteed to run smoothly for eight days with no need for rewinding. Such innovations are nothing new where the Reverso is concerned: there is a long tradition of enamellers and engravers using its second face to turn the watch into a unique objet d'art, while Jaeger-LeCoultre's designers have also used the watch back to delight devotees of horological complications by showing a second function.

The Atmos Clock

Jaeger-LeCoultre has had a special relationship with the present monarch since her coronation day, when the young Queen chose to wear the Calibre 101, the world's tiniest mechanical wristwatch movement, developed by Jaeger-LeCoultre in 1929, at her Coronation at Westminster Abbey in 1952

As such, it seems appropriate that the Swiss watchmakers should have chosen to mark the Queen's Golden Jubilee this year with a horological marvel. The tradition of monarchy reigning in the British Isles spans over a millennium now, so to match the regal institution's extraordinary longevity Jaeger-LeCoultre has produced a special Golden Jubilee thousand-year Atmos clock.

Engraved with the royal coat of arms and names of all the British kings and queens since 802, these extraordinary thousand year clocks have been engineered to display the time, date, year and moon phase until the end of the millennium. One of these very exclusive clocks will be offered to Her Majesty The Queen as an official Golden Jubilee gift during the Royal Windsor Horse Show in May 2002.

Jaeger-LeCoultre has produced the Atmos Golden Jubilee in two limited editions of just 50 pieces. Purchasers of this rare horological masterpiece will be in very select company indeed.

Note from the editor: To reserve one of these historic and highly exclusive Golden Jubilee Atmos Clocks, please contact Richard Shirley at the Jaeger-LeCoultre Boutique – 1A Old Bond Street – London W1 – Tel:020 7538 8070

It is no accident that Jaeger-LeCoultre is able to maintain such high technical and aesthetic standards. The secret lies, of course, in the company's unbending commitment to excellence and innovation. The modest little farm workshop in Le Sentier established nearly two centuries ago by Antoine LeCoultre now employs 900 skilled people, and Jaeger-LeCoultre is almost unique in the watchmaking world in having the capacity and know-how to hand-manufacture every single component of its timepieces itself – rare qualities in today's brand-saturated, marketing-led global economy, where image is so often considered more important than substance.

The Jaeger-LeCoultre story is a remarkable one, and one that the Swiss watchmakers are now determined to tell through their Old Bond Street boutique. The company has always enjoyed a special relationship with Britain: it was in Antoine LeCoultre's lifetime that it forged its first links here, when the judges at the 1851 Great Exhibition in Paxton's Crystal Palace awarded LeCoultre a gold medal for his innovative chronometer with a new keyless winding and setting system. Nor is the Great Exhibition the only occasion on which the company has participated in a historic event on these shores. Just over a century later, in 1953, it played a discreet role in the coronation of Elizabeth II, when the young queen opted to wear the Calibre 101 – the world's tiniest mechanical wristwatch movement, developed by Jaeger-LeCoultre in 1929 – while she prepared to don the imperial crown in Westminster Abbey.

Above left: Jaeger-LeCoultre Boutique's watchmaker Richard Phipps-Carter, seen at work

Above top: A bespoke engraved Reverso

Above bottom: Portrait of Sir Winston Churchill with the Atmos Clock

Above: Reverso
Septantième

Above right: Golden
Jubillee Atmos Clock,
Reverso Pink

This year, one great institution honours another
when Jaeger-LeCoultre launches its limited-edition
Atmos Golden Jubilee clock to celebrate the 50th
anniversary of Her Majesty The Queen's Accession
to the Throne.

To reflect the Triumph of a thousand years of a
monarchy in the British Isles, the cabinet of each
clock has been meticulously inscribed with the royal
coat of arms and the names and dates of all British
kings and queens since 802, the year in which King
Egbert came to power.

Building on the unique heritage it so faithfully
perpetuates, the Manufacture Jaeger–LeCoultre
cultivates and develops the technical mastery and
culture of time measurement. Its reference is its
own experience: its past guides it towards the
future in the quest for successful mergers between
watchmaking tradition and fine craftmanship.

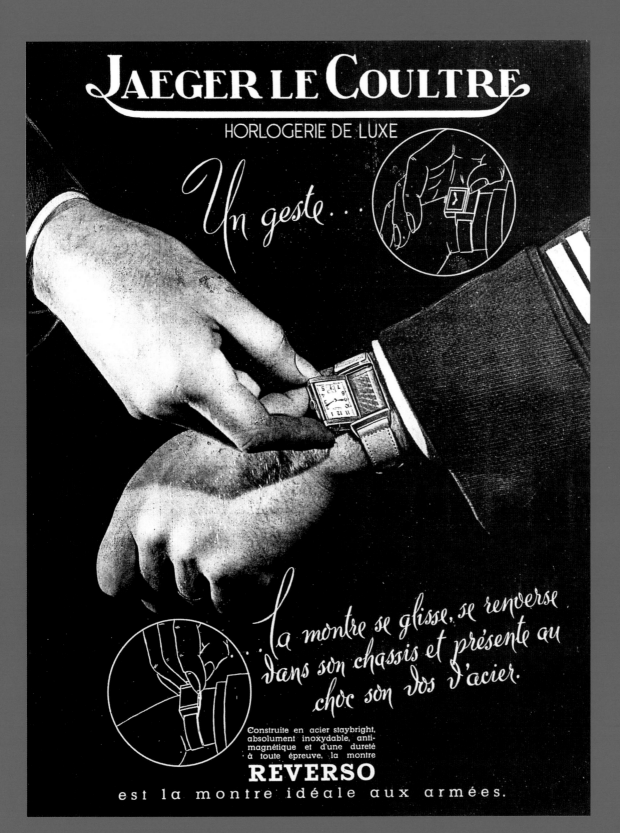

JAEGER LE COULTRE

HORLOGERIE DE LUXE

Un geste...

...la montre se glisse, se renverse dans son chassis et présente au choc son dos d'acier.

Construite en acier staybright, absolument inoxydable, anti-magnétique et d'une dureté à toute épreuve, la montre

REVERSO

est la montre idéale aux armées.

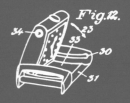

The Queen as a Racehorse Owner and Breeder

As a leading owner and breeder of racehorses the Queen is maintaining a tradition of four centuries and indeed the history of the Royal Studs is closely interwoven with the evolution of the thoroughbred. Racing is recorded in the reign of Elizabeth I while James I and Charles I sponsored the importation of stallions and mares from the Middle East to improve the native running horses, resulting in the development of the modern racehorse.

Charles I and Queen Anne did much to establish the racecourses at New market and Ascot, George II's son William Duke of Cumberland bred the unbeaten Eclipse from whom over 90% of all thoroughbreds descend while George IV had great success with the his stud at Hampton Court.

Queen Victoria is never associated with racing but it is a fact that during her reign the Royal Stud at Hampton Court was the most influential in England and she was the first person to breed the winners of the Derby and the Oaks in the same year while in La Fleche she bred the greatest racemare of the 19th century.

Kind Edward VII established the studs at Sandringham and Wolferton in Norfolk and won the Derby three times with the home - bred full brothers Permission and Diamond Jubilee and with Minouri which he leased. George V maintained a keen interest in the royal racing and breeding tradition and in his reign the great foudation mare Feola joined the stud which, when The Queen inherited it from King George VI, was of the highest class and included the brilliant classic winner Hypericum, a daughter of Feola.

As a girl The Queen always greatly enjoyed her visits to the studs and to the royal horses in training at Newmarket and Beckhampton in Wiltshire and

soon became very knowledgable. The first horse to carry her colours as Princess Elizabeth was the steeplechaser Monaveen which she owned in partnership with her mother Queen Elizabeth, now the highly successful and best loved patron of racing over jumps. In coronation year The Queen's Aureole, a grandson of Feola, was second in the Derby to Pinza ridden by Sir Gordon Richards and went on to be an outstanding four year old.

The Queen's broodmares, numbering about 25, were kept at Hampton Court and at the Sandringham and Wolferton studs in Norfolk, with the weaned foals going to Ireland for a year before returning to England to be broken in and trained. Since the early seventies the weaned foals have been kept at the Polhampton Lodge stud near Kingsclere in Berkshire. For almost the first 20 years of The Queen's reign her horses were trained at Newmarket by Captain Sir Cecil Boyd-Rochfort, a celebrated master of his profession. He was succeeded by the highly successful trainers Major Dick Hern at West Ilsey in Berkshire and Ian Balding at Kingsclere. The stallions kept at Sandringham and Wolferton were visited each year by mares from all over the world. Aureole, who stood at the Wolferton Stud was a highly successful stallion and twice became Champion sire.

The first decade of The Queen's reign was a particularly glorious period for the Royal Studs. In 1954 Aureole went on to win the Coronation Cup, the Hardwick Stakes at Royal Ascot and the highly prestigious King George VI and Queen Elizabeth Stakes at Ascot in July. Almeria won the Yorkshire Oaks, the Park Hill Stakes and Doncaster Cup and was the best staying filly of her day. Pall Mall won the classic Two Thousand Guineas in 1958 and became a successful sire.

Top: The Queen enjoying a day's racing with her beloved late mother, HM Queen Elizabeth the Queen Mother, whose passion for racing was just as intense

Far left: The Queen photographed at Balmoral in 1972 by Lord Lichfield

Other high class winners bred by The Queen in the 1950s included High Veldt, Doutelle, Restoration and Above Suspicion. Doutelle and Above Suspicion did well as stallions while High Veldt became leading sire in South Africa. At the same descendants of mares at the Royal Studs were having great influence overseas, the then world record prize money winner Round Table being another grandson of Feola.

All studs tend to ride peaks and troughs and the 1960s were a relatively quiet time for Queen's racing. A high point was the Eclipse Stakes win of Canisbay. Later leading sire in Italy while Crest of the Wave became Champion sire in New Zealand. Gaulois and Castle Yard were other leading winners at this time. Until the late 1960s yearlings bred at the National Stud were leased to race by The Queen and included top class performers like Pindari, Landau and Hopeful Venture.

In spite of the growing competition from some of the best American-bred horses bought as yearlings to race in Europe the 1970s were another golden decade for The Queen's horses. Example, in her year the best staying filly in Europe, Magna Carta, Charlton and Albany were leading lights in The Queen's racing team when, in 1974, a real star arrived in the shape of Highclere. This big, long striding filly and a great granddaughter of Feola, won the classic one thousand Guineas at Newmarket and then scored a brilliant triumph in the Prix de Diane, the French Oaks. A possibly even better filly emerged in 1977, the year of The Queen's Silver Jubilee, when Dunfermline won the Oaks and then the St. Leger when she became the only horse ever to beat Alleged, twice winner of the Prix de l'Arc de Triomphe Escorial.

The Queen showing obvious pleasure **(left)** at the races and **(right)** admiring one of her horses

Far left: The Queen with (left) Princess Margaret and (right) the late Queen Mother at Epsom, 1958

Above: At Badminton Horse Trials with her camera at the ready

Although The Queen had kept at least one mare in the United States since the late 1960s by the 1980s so many of the World's best stallions were in Kentucky that it was decided to increase the number of mares mated there each year to five or six. These were divided between Dr. and Mrs John Chandler's Mill Ridge Farm and Lane's End Farm, both in Lexington, the mecca of American bloodstock breeding. Lana's End belongs to Mr William S. Farris, the American Ambassador to this country and a friend of The Queen who was his guest for the four private visits she has made to see her mares and foals and the stallions they were visiting. When weaned the foals are flown back to spend the next year with the other yearlings at the Polhampton Stud.

Aureole was succeeded at Wolferton in 1977 by another great racehorse and fine stallion in the St. Leger winner Bustino, bred and raced by the Late Lady Beaverbrook and owned at stud by a syndicate of breeders. Two years later Shirley Heights, winner of the Epsom and Irish Derbies, came to stand at Sandringham. Bred and raced by Lord Halifax and his late father and owned at stud by a syndicate, Shirley Heights became an even more successful and influential stallion.

By the 1980s racing and breeding had become even more internationalised with increasing competition from horses bred overseas, particularly in America. The Arab owner-breeders had arrived on the scene, operating to the very highest standards but on a scale far larger than had ever seen before and completely dwarfing The Queen's stud and

racing stable. The royal horses continued to enjoy plenty of success, however, without seriously challenging the domination of the classic races by the four Maktoum brothers from Dubai, Prince Khaled Abdullah and the Aga Khan each of whom operate on a scale some ten times larger than The Queen and backed by an investment far greater still.

Soprano, Highbrow and Starlet were good winners in the 1980s while unknown Quantity went over to Chicago for the important Arlington Handicap Stakes and won. Height of fashion, a daughter of Bustino and Highclere and even bigger than her mother was the leading two year old filly of 1981. When sold after her racing career to Sheikh Hamdan al Maktoum she became one of the world's greatest broodmares. Six of her foals have become top class racehorses including Nashwan, winner of the Two Thousand Guineas, Derby, Eclipse Stakes and King George VI and Queen Elizabeth Stakes and the highly successful stallion Unfuwain.

Major Hern was succeeded at West Ilsley in the mid-1980s by Lord Huntingdon and today The Queen's trainers are Sir Michael Stoute at Newmarket, Roger Charlton at Beckhampton and Richard Hannon at East Everleigh. The Queen's interest in her studs and the horses in training remain as close as ever. When she can she loves to visit the studs to see the mares and foals at Sandringham and the yearlings at Polhampton. However, her duties prevent her making these visits as often as she would like and her Stud Manager keeps her informed of all important events such as the arrival of a foal and sends video film to show

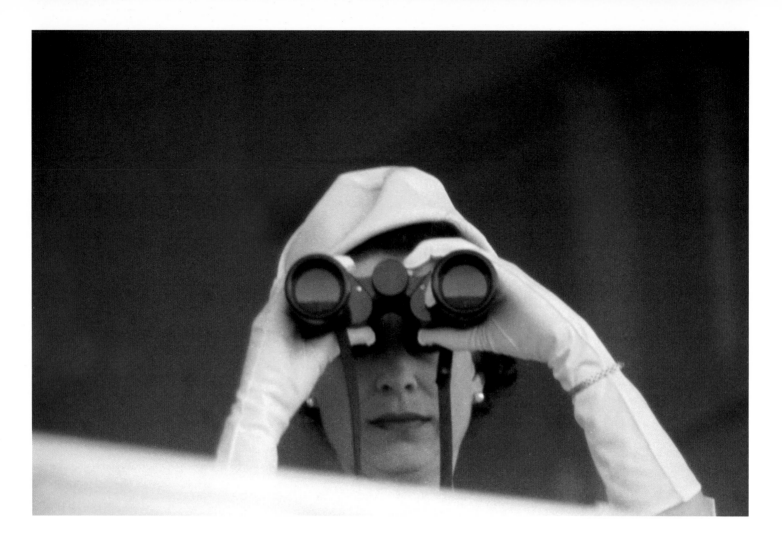

Top: The Queen watching racing at Lahore Racecourse on her tour of Pakistan, February 1961

how the young stock are progressing. The Queen has an encyclopaedic knowledge of pedigrees and her Stud Manager - Sir Michael Oswald from 1970 to 1998 and now Joe Grimwade - needs to do his homework on each sales catalogue as it appears if he wants to keep up. No important decision is taken without her approval and to all intents and purposes The Queen is the manager.

As with the studs, the Queen's duties prevent her racing when she would like to see her horses run - she had to miss the two classic victories of Dunfermline - although some major race meetings like the Derby, Royal Ascot and the King George VI and Queen Elizabeth Stakes are ring fenced in her diary. Her Racing Manager, the Earl of Carnavon from 1970 until his sudden death last September, has always kept her in touch with all developments and her trainers are in direct telephone contact, reporting on each race while today television and video managers to see the yearlings at Polhampton, watch her horses on the training gallops the next morning followed by a runner and, with luck, a winner in the afternoon.

The Royal Studs are run as a strictly commercial business and not one penny of public money is involved; to afford to buy something, something else may have to be sold. Although unable to compete on anything like level terms with the big battalions The Queen's horses are winning plenty of good races and, in fact, the years 1992-1994 were the best ever in terms of winners bred and number of races won. Last year her filly Flight of Fancy, despite a very rough passage in the race, was second in the Oaks and considered unlucky not to have won.

The Queen has won some 650 races as an owner and has bred the winners of over a thousand. Her enthusiasm and knowledge of all aspects of "the Sport of Kings" should ensure more success in the years to come to carry on the great tradition of the Royal Studs.

How would you feel if your horse went missing? Alarmed? Angry? Guilty?

When horse thieves strike, the effect is devastating. Which is why so many owners seek the protection of a Farmkey freezemark, together with the peace of mind it brings.

Over the past 22 years we've protected one out of three of the country's horses with our freezemark. So there's little we don't know about the subject.

To find out more just give us a call. It's the very least you can do for your horse.

0870 870 7107
www.farmkey.co.uk

Established 1978

BY APPOINTMENT TO HER MAJESTY THE QUEEN
FOR HORSE FREEZE MARKING SECURITY SERVICES

Farmkey, Westmere Drive, Crewe, Cheshire CW1 6ZY
Email info@farmkey.co.uk

FARM|KEY

Message from the US Ambassador

Sarah and I send our warmest greetings to all those involved in producing this tribute to a great monarch, and a great horsewoman.

As Sir Michael notes in the preceding chapter, those who know about horses seem to feel that Kentucky produces most of the world's best stallions. We Kentuckians are proud of our reputation, and we are doubly proud to see it recognized by the greatest horsepeople around the world. The Kentucky Derby, the Keenland sales, and the Kentucky breeding industry – with more than 1,000 farms in and around Lexington, all leaders in their particular specialty – combine to make the thoroughbred horse a state symbol.

The American people are delighted to join with our best friends, the British people, in celebrating the Golden Jubilee of Queen Elizabeth II

Bill Farish

SSAFA FORCES *Help*

The Soldiers, Sailors, Airmen and Families Association – Forces Help
The national charity helping serving and ex-Service men, women and their families, in need.

ATQH 01/02

Our forces are for life, not just for war

For over 100 years SSAFA Forces Help has been helping serving and ex-Service men, women and their families in need. Our priority is people, and our commitment is to provide practical and emotional help and support to anyone who has served just one paid day in any of our three armed forces, including the Reserves, and their families.

We estimate that one quarter of the population could be eligible for our help. Every year our 7,000 volunteers help over 85,000 people. Help us to help those that served for you.

By making a bequest to SSAFA Forces Help, you'll give us the will to make a difference.

Nominated Charity

If you would like to receive our **FREE Legacy Fact File**, make a donation, leave a gift in your will or to find out more about our organisation please contact us:
**SSAFA Forces Help, 19 Queen Elizabeth Street, London SE1 2LP
Tel: 020 7403 8783 E-mail: info@ssafa.org.uk
Website: www.ssafa.org.uk**

Registered Charity No. 210760. Established 1885

The Household Cavalry

During great royal and state occasions in British history, the horse has often played a significant role. The Household Cavalry provides the Sovereign's personal mounted escort on state occasions. The Household Cavalry is the collective title given to the two senior regiments of the British Army, the Life Guards, and the Blues and Royals. The Lifeguards were formed by King Charles II some weeks prior to his restoration to the throne in 1660; the Royal Horse Guards (The Blues) was originally a parliamentary cavalry regiment raised in the north-east in 1650 and, ten years later, joined those parliamentary forces supporting the King's return to the throne. Today, both the Life Guards and the Blues and Royals man two of Britain's most modern regiments, equipped with either the latest main battle tanks or armoured reconnaissance vehicles. In addition, both regiments together form the small ceremonial regiment known officially as the Mounted Regiment, which escorts the Queen on horseback on official state and royal occasions.

The King's Troop Royal Horse Artillery are also Household Troops. Their duties include the firing of royal salutes in Hyde Park on royal anniversaries and state occasions, and providing a gun carriage and teams of black horses for state and military funerals. The King's Troop also takes part in other ceremonial occasions, such as Armistice Day, the Lord Mayor's Show and the Queen's Birthday Parade. In addition, it performs the duties of the Queen's Life Guard at Whitehall for one month each year.

Before the Second World War, a succession of horse artillery batteries were stationed in London. It was King George VI's express wish that, after the war, a troop of Royal Horse Artillery, mounted and dressed in the traditional manner, should once more take part in the great ceremonies of state. In 1947,

His Majesty announced that he wished the Riding Troop to be known as His Troop, and the Queen decided that this title should continue in recognition of her beloved father's special interest in 'The Troop'. Even today, the King's Troop firing a royal salute is one of the most spectacular ceremonies to be seen in the heart of London; 71 horses take part, and the officers and soldiers wear their colourful ceremonial dress. The six guns form up in a line abreast in Hyde Park and gallop into action. A salute of 41 guns is then fired and as the last round echoes across the park, the guns are hooked into their teams of horses and they gallop away. During the summer, The Troop performs its Musical Drive at various agricultural shows and military tattoos up and down the country. The drive, which has been performed in a number of overseas cities, is an exciting and spectacular display of horsemanship, carried out at the gallop, and culminating in the dangerous scissor movement when teams cross in the centre of the arena with the minimum space between them.

The Troop boasts 111 horses, nearly all of which come from Ireland. The majority arrive as five year olds, and are hacked at Melton Mowbray for ten weeks or so and then trained at St John's Wood in London. Today, over one-third of the King's Troop horses take part in horse trials, hunter trials and showjumping events in Britain, and win many prizes. There have also been a number of horses and riders in the King's Troop who have taken part in various Olympic Games. Most soldiers who join the King's Troop do so because of their interest in horses, but others want to work as saddlers, farriers, tailors, vehicle drivers or orderlies. All have the opportunity to learn to ride. Those who work exclusively with the horses are given intensive riding and horsemanship instruction, and all have the responsibility of looking after their own horse in the stables.

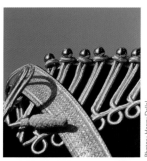

Above: Accoutrements of the Household Cavalry

Left: Rehearsing for the Queen's Annual Birthday Parade on Horse Guards Parade in the early hours

Above: Preparing the horses hooves

Right: Fitting a harness at Knightsbridge Barracks, the home of the Household Cavalry in London

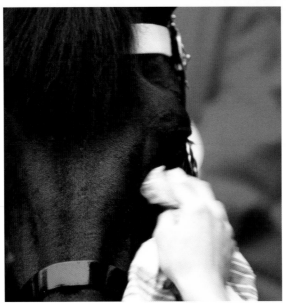

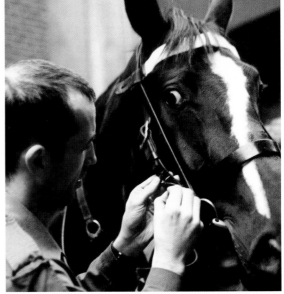

Photos: Henry Dallal

It was not until the mid-18th century that 'true' cavalry - fast, light horses of great stamina - were employed, with their ability to launch lightning attacks. True cavalry in great masses were used in nearly all European wars of the 19th century, but during the course of the Franco-Prussian War of 1871 the end of the horse as the magnificent, all-conquering war machine was to be signalled by the arrival on the field of battle of the deadly Montigny machine gun.

In Britain, the courage, tenacity and boldness of the horse will forever be remembered in the immortal words of Alfred Lord Tennyson in his stirring and evocative poem The Charge of the Light Brigade, in which the Royal Horse Guards took part.

Historically, the first personal mounted guard was formed back in 1509 by Henry VIII. They were known as the Band of Gentleman Spears because the spear was the only weapon they carried. Later, the title was changed to the Honourable Corps of Gentlemen at Arms. Those 50 recruits to Henry VIII's personal cavalry, who were ordered to own three large draught horses each and a groom, were recruited from the landed gentry. Today, however, the Corps of Gentlemen at Arms is no longer mounted.

The Royal Horse Guards (The Blues) were first raised in 1650 prior to Cromwell's second invasion of Scotland. The Life Guards - some 80 Royalists - was raised ten years later, just before the restoration of King Charles II, as his personal

ROYAL ASCOT
Greater than ever for 2002

This year, Royal Ascot promises to be the most spectacular ever.
Extended to five days to celebrate The Queen's Golden Jubilee, there's no better opportunity to experience the splendour, pageantry and excitement of this famous event. Tickets are selling fast so book now to guarantee your place at this summer's greatest sporting and social occasion.

Tuesday 18th – Saturday 22nd June

Book now on 01344 876 876 or www.ascot.co.uk

bodyguard. The Royal Dragoons (1st Dragoons) trace their origins to a troop of horse raised by Charles II in 1661. Both guards regiments fought with distinction in many famous English battles during the next 300 years, including the War of the Austrian Succession the 1740, the Seven Years War, the Peninsular Campaign of 1813-14, and under the command of the Duke of Wellington at the Battle of Waterloo in 1815.

The Household Cavalry fought in Egypt and the Sudan in the 1880s, and in the Boer War in South Africa at the turn of the century. They later spent some nine years in India. The regiment also played a pivotal role throughout the First World War and, in the Second World War, were heavily involved in North Africa and after the Allied landing in France.

After the Second World War, and the final departure of the horse in favour of mechanisation, a composite regiment known as the Household Cavalry Mounted Regiment, based at Hyde Park Barracks, was formed to carry out public duties. This regiment consists of two sabre squadrons. With 250 horses, it is the regiment's task to carry out the traditional role of the Household Cavalry; its duties include providing the Queen's Life Guard daily at Horse Guards, finding all the sovereign's escorts, providing massed mounted bands, and certain dismounted duties for the Royal Family and visiting heads of state. It was in 1969 that the Blues

Photos: Henry Dallal

Right: After a rehearsal for Trooping the Colour 2001

Top: Preparing for the state visit of the King of Jordan in November 2001 at Windsor Castle

Bottom: Christmas hijinks at Knightsbridge Barracks

and Royals were eventually amalgamated to form a new regiment within the Household Cavalry.

The famous Band of the Life Guards goes back to 1660 when the mounted bandsmen played their kettledrums and trumpets as King Charles II rode into London escorted by his Life Guards. Today, the band has 36 musicians and they all ride black horses of some 16 hands, except for the drummer who, by tradition, rides a piebald or skewbald horse of some 17 hands or more.

In 1992 the new-look Household Cavalry Regiment, comprising two squadrons of Life Guards and two squadrons of Blues and Royals, was formed, although despite the union each regiment has retained its separate identity, uniforms, traditions and standards. The Colonel-in-Chief of each Regiment is Her Majesty the Queen; indeed, since 1821, all Colonels-in-Chief have, by tradition, been the reigning monarch.

FARLOWS

FARLOWS OF PALL MALL - AHEAD OF THE FIELD FOR 160 YEARS.
COUNTRY CLOTHING, FISHING TACKLE, SHOOTING ACCESSORIES
5 PALL MALL, LONDON SW1Y 5NP, TEL: 020 7839 2423, WWW.FARLOWS.CO.UK

Henry Dallal is a landscape photographer and mountaineer, who has spent the last 5 years intimately photographing the life of the Household Cavalry. His work has been exhibited at Kensington Palace and he is currently working on soon to be published books on the Household Cavalry and the King's Troop Royal Horse Artillery. He uses a style of photography that tries to capture the spirit and theme of Pageantry and Performance. Henry has been especially commissioned to photograph Her Majesty The Queen for the front cover of this magazine.

Hdallal@yahoo.com
www.henrydallal.com

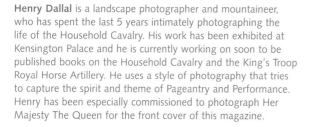

Photos: Henry Dallal

All Freemasons under the United Grand Lodge of England send loyal and heartfelt congratulations to Her Majesty Queen Elizabeth II on the occasion of The Golden Jubilee

United Grand Lodge of England
HRH The Duke of Kent, KG
Grand Master

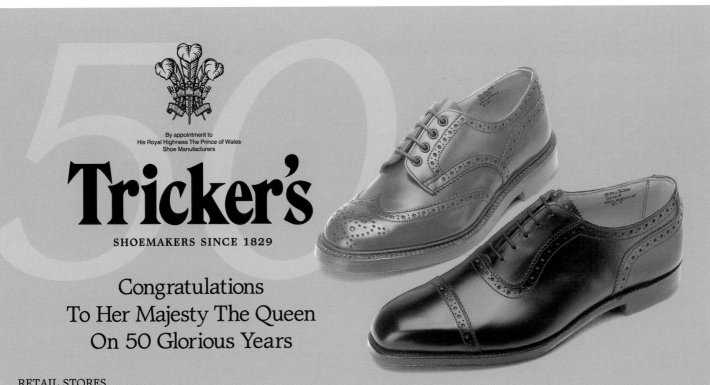

By appointment to
His Royal Highness The Prince of Wales
Shoe Manufacturers

Tricker's

SHOEMAKERS SINCE 1829

Congratulations
To Her Majesty The Queen
On 50 Glorious Years

RETAIL STORES

67 Jermyn Street
St James's, London SW1
Tel: 020 7930 6395

117 Newgate Street
London EC1A

18 Market Place
Pickering, N. Yorks, YO18
Tel: 01751 474486

www.trickers.com

The Royal Mews

The elegant grey horses that pull the magnificent royal coaches are without doubt the most celebrated and most exclusive team of carriage horses in the world. They are hand-picked from around Britain and Ireland, trained to the highest level and, when being driven, they are as near perfect as horses can be - constant, precise and sure-footed. These greys are the horses seen on television screens throughout Britain and across the world during great State occasions with their marble coats, their noble heads, their perfect action, their swishing tails and their flawless behaviour. To see these greys at work, harnessed to one of the magnificent Royal coaches trotting down the Mall or down the course at Royal Ascot is to see horses that have been trained as a team with great patience, diligence and expertise.

The Royal greys – owned by the Queen – live in the comfort of the Royal Mews next to Buckingham Palace but they work far harder than many would assume. In addition to being star attractions on state occasions these greys also trot around London most mornings pulling a small brougham – a one horse, closed carriage - taking a Queen's messenger from place to place delivering and picking up mail. Indeed, delivering the Queen's mail between the various Royal residences in London, provides valuable training exercises for both horse and coachman. When those responsible for keeping an eye on the Royal finances took a close look at the Royal Mews in the 1990s they suggested streamlining the place by putting an end to the daily delivery of mail by horse and carriage and modernising the operation. Before this new-fangled idea was put into operation it was pointed out that the royal brougham was used not only to deliver the mail but also to train horses and young coachmen. The idea was dropped and Londoners still have the joy of seeing the immaculate blue brougham pulled by a grey or a bay trotting around London's crowded streets seemingly impervious to the noise, rush and bustle of the traffic.

As well as the Greys, which are generally reserved for the exclusive use of the Queen, there are also the lovely Cleveland bays which are also used on a daily basis. These are generally harnessed when called to perform duties such as taking other celebrities and distinguished visitors, such as ambassadors, to and from Buckingham Palace. The daily routine of the Queen's horses hardly ever varies. At 6.30 each morning, while their stables are being cleaned and fresh straw put down, they are harnessed, usually in pairs to brakes, and taken out for their first exercise of the day around the streets of London which usually lasts about for an hour. For those Londoners who rise early enough they see the horses enjoying their morning exercise; an exhilarating experience for the horses lend a touch of country life to the tarmac and tall buildings of the capital. Regular work in harness is vital to keep their shoulders hard otherwise the skin may become soft and skin sores may then occur.

After exercising hard and sometimes cantering quite fast around London's streets the horses return for their breakfast followed by the first grooming of the day, including a thorough washing. By the time the grooms have completed that job on all the horses in their care the morning is all but over. During some part of the day, the greys and bays which share the superb, high-roofed stables listen to loud music and the sound of loud bands, drums and military music can be heard wafting from the Royal Mews which, of course, keeps the horses used to the sound of martial music. On some occasions flags and banners are waved in front of them, scarves and gloves thrown into the air and the noise of cheering crowds and martial music is turned up to full volume so that the Royal horses come to accept such noise and mayhem as simply a part of their everyday life.

The horses receive their second feed of the day at midday and another meal at five in the afternoon.

Top: The Queen visits the Indoor Riding School in the Royal Mews

Bottom: The Queen and Princess Anne

Above: A view of the stables in the Royal Mews

Sometimes they are fed simply hay, at other times some hard feed, such as a few horse nuts, are provided depending on their workload and the horse's own individual appetite. At about 6 pm in the winter months their dark blue rugs embroidered with the Crown are removed and plain night rugs put on. Sometimes some of the horses are given an extra feed at eight o'clock and then they settle down for the night.

The training of the Royal greys is a long, patient and painstaking process. Most come to the Royal Mews at five or six years of age for a trial to see if those responsible for training them believe they would be suitable for the job. When they pass that initial, trial examination they are handed to a 'rough-rider' teasingly so called because those riders are the opposite of rough. All horses begin their education in the indoor riding school – a large hangar-style building - inside the Mews. Hanging from the roof's metal girders are large flags of different colours so that from the very beginning a horse becomes accustomed to them hanging and moving above his head. First, a long reign is attached to a ring in the bridle and not to a bit. This long reign exercise is used to teach the young pupil to walk at a set pace, to trot, turn or stop at the slightest touch of the rein. Only after the grey has mastered this to the satisfaction of the rough-rider is a double rein introduced, attached to each side of the horse's head. This is to train the horse to accept being steered. These two training exercises sometimes take a couple of months to ensure the horse is totally at ease with both disciplines.

The pupil is then introduced to an older grey which is brought into the school to show the younger grey how things should be done. The two horses are harnessed together and the younger one learns what he must and must not do when working with a partner. The idea works wonderfully well and in most circumstances the young horse learns remarkably quickly.

The next lesson teaches the young horse to accept that he has to work for his living not simply trot around an indoor ring. And work means pulling heavy coaches. The weight of the heaviest, the wonderful Gold State Coach used for Coronations is an incredible four tons! Now, the novice horse is harnessed in a team of four with his older partner next to him. During this phase of learning the young horse has to understand that the reins are controlled either from the coachman on top, as is the Irish Coach, or by the postillion on his companion's back, as is the case with the golden State Coach or the State Landau. After that hurdle is safely passed, the novice is tried as one of six such as the number required to pull the State Landau or as one of eight for the superb Gold Coach. He is placed in various positions in the team until it is judged he could be tested at even more advanced work. He is harnessed as a wheeler, the place of honour, being one of the horses immediately in front of the coach. It is the wheelers with the twelve foot long carriage pole between them which are the bedrock of a successful team. If and when he passes that ultimate test the novice will then become one of the Queen's own royal greys.

The wheelers are responsible for 'taking the strain' in preparation for moving off - helped by the horses in front - while the wheelers are actually standing still. When the order is given to 'move off' only a small additional effort is then needed to get under way. Stopping the four-ton coach is an awesome and difficult manoeuvre and this, more than any other controlled movement, is the most tense and anxious moment for the coachmen. It is the responsibility of the wheelers alone. Some ten yards before the halting point the postilion slows them a fraction at a time, the other horses stop pulling, and gradually the weight of the coach presses upon the breechings round the wheelers' powerful haunches. As the burden increases, the wheelers plant their feet more firmly and exert their strength by infinite degrees until the coach comes to a halt.

BY APPOINTMENT TO
HER MAJESTY THE QUEEN.
MANUFACTURERS OF WATERPROOF
AND PROTECTIVE CLOTHING
J. BARBOUR & SONS LTD.,
SOUTH SHIELDS.

BY APPOINTMENT TO
H.R.H. THE DUKE OF EDINBURGH.
MANUFACTURERS OF WATERPROOF
AND PROTECTIVE CLOTHING
J. BARBOUR & SONS LTD.,
SOUTH SHIELDS.

BY APPOINTMENT TO
H.R.H. THE PRINCE OF WALES.
MANUFACTURERS OF WATERPROOF
AND PROTECTIVE CLOTHING
J. BARBOUR & SONS LTD.,
SOUTH SHIELDS.

www.barbour.com

Barbour ®

FOR BROCHURE AND STOCKISTS CALL FREEPHONE 0800 009988

Top: Shining bridles and saddles in the Tack Room

Bottom: The Coachmen's livery is covered in gold braid

Right: The Farrier attends the Queen's Horses at the Royal Mews

Opposite Page: Coaches are a regular mode of transport for the Queen

In the days of Queen Victoria the situation was even more of a nightmare for the coachman and postilions because the gold coach then had no brakes and no brakeman walking behind which meant that the full weight of the coach was being taken on the back legs of the wheelers. Going downhill was described as a 'nightmare' but there is no mention of any disasters or accidents.

At first, the youngster is given experience on the less demanding occasions, helping to draw the Queen's carriage at Royal Ascot for example of as part of a team transporting a distinguished visitor to Buckingham Palace. Only when his trainers are totally satisfied that the novice has become of age and has enough basic experience will he be permitted to draw a state coach on a major occasions such as the Queen's birthday or the State Opening of Parliament. These are the occasions when the novice will see the flags flying everywhere, thousands of people watching the royal spectacle and the noise of both martial music, cheering crowds, the roar of London's traffic and sometimes the incessant 'clack-clack-clack' of noisy helicopters overhead.

Throughout all this the greys must remain calm no matter what happens. The great majority of the Royal greys and the bays are geldings, not mares, because experience has shown that mares are less steady than geldings when confronted by noise and general hullabaloo. The principal ceremonial coaches and carriages – garaged in the Royal Mews - to which the Royal greys are harnessed include the State Landau, built in 1902 for King Edward V11

which requires six greys and two outriders; the Irish State Coach, so called as it was designed by the then Lord Mayor of Dublin, a coachbuilder, and bought by Queen Victoria in 1852 which requires four harnessed greys and two outriders; The small Glass Coach, perhaps the most graceful of all the Royal carriages, needs only a pair.

But, it is the superb heavyweight gold Coronation Coach, which was originally built for King George 111 in 1761, which needs a full team of eight strong greys. This was last used at the Queen's Silver Jubilee in June 1977 to carry the Queen and Prince Philip to the Thanksgiving Service at St. Paul's Cathedral. The framework of the body of this remarkable coach consists of eight palm trees which, branching at the top, support the roof. The four corner trees, each rising from a lion's head, are loaded with trophies symbolising the victories of Great Britain in the Seven Years War that ended just after the coach was built. The body is slung by braces covered in morocco leather and ornamented with gilt buckles held by four tritons. On the cntre of the roof stand three cherubs representing the genii of England, Scotland and Ireland. These support the Royal Crown and hold in their hands the Sceptre and the Ensign of Knighthood. Their bodies are draped with festoons of laurel which fall to the four corners of the roof.

Other minor features include the driver's footboard in the shape of a large scallop shell ornamented with bunches of reeds; the pole representing a bundle of lances; the splinter bar

composed of a rich moulding issuing from beneath a large spiral shell with each end terminating in a dolphin's head; and the wheels copied from those of an ancient triumphal car. The coach is gilded all over. It is 24 feet long, 8 feet 3 inches wide and 12 feet high. The pole is 12 feet 4 inches long and the harness is of rich morocco leather. The side, front and back panels were painted by Giovanni Battista Cipriani, a Florentine historical painter and engraver who came to London in 1755.

Other Royal coaches include the Scottish State Coach, in seniority the third state coach, which was once owned by Princess Mary of Adelaide, Duchess of Teck. It was later sold to the Earl of Albermarle, altered to an open landau and subsequently given to Queen Mary in 1930.The coach is emblazoned with the royal arms for Scotland and the insignia of the Order of the Thistle. In 1969 a new top was fitted and given two large glass windows and a unique feature – two transparent panels in the roof, not only to provide extra light but also to enable spectators on high to see the occupants of the coach. The Scottish State Coach is the lightest, brightest and many consider the most elegant. There is also Queen Alexandra's State Coach built in 1865 and converted into a 'glass state coach' in 1893 for the Princess of Wales, later Queen Alexandra.

One of the newest is the Australian State Coach presented to the Queen in Canberra in 1988 as a gift from the Australian people to celebrate Australia's bi-centennial year. This coach is of similar design to the Irish State Coach and may be drawn by six or four horses, postilion ridden. However, the Australian State Coach has a hidden advantage over all the other coaches: it is the only coach boasting central heating and electric windows! In all the other coaches, water bottles bought from Boots, the Chemists are secreted beneath beautiful embroidered covers. Until the 1990s, all the hot water bottles were copper but the 21st century beckoned and it was decided a job lot of new water-bottles should be purchased.

And then there is the beautiful, romantic Glass Coach, used for nearly all Royal weddings, which generally takes the bride and bridegroom from Clarence House to their weddings. The Queen as Princess Elizabeth rode in the Glass Coach for her marriage to Prince Philip in 1947 and for Princess Anne when she married Captain Mark Phillips in 1973. Lady Diana Spencer and Miss Sarah Ferguson also travelled from Clarence House to their weddings in the same coach.

The State Landaus were introduced in the middle of the nineteenth century when the introduction of railways made the building of strong coaches for long hard journeys unnecessary. They were made much lighter and no larger than necessary. These are generally drawn by two bay horses driven from the box.Every year, television news records the Queen's procession up the course at Royal Ascot, when she arrives each day in an Ascot landau with members of the family or other guests. There are five of these elegant, lightweight postilion landaus and they are kept at the Royal Mews at Windsor Castle.

Chronology of the Queen's Reign

1952
King George VI dies
Queen Elizabeth II ascends the throne

1953
Queen Elizabeth's Coronation
The Queen is crowned in Westminster Abbey

1953 - 54
Commonwealth Royal Tour
The Queen establishes her special relationship
with the Commonwealth

1955
Churchill retires
The Queen dines at 10 Downing Street

1956
The Queen visits Nigeria
The Queen cements her relationship with
the Commonwealth

1957
First tv christmas
The first transmission of The Queen's
Christmas Message takes place on television

1959
Birth of Prince Andrew
The Queen's family has always been of supreme
importance

1960
The Queen's sister marries
Princess Margaret marries Anthony Armstrong-Jones

1962
Commonwealth meeting
Queen attends Commonwealth Heads of
Government meeting in London as Head of the
Commonwealth.

1963
**President John Kennedy
assassinated**
The Queen expresses the British people's deep sense
of shock

1964
Birth of Prince Edward
The Queen's fourth and last child completes
her family

1965
Rhodesia declares UDI
The monarchy remains aloof from the crisis

1966
The Aberfan disaster
146 men, women and children killed

1967
Pacific Commonwealth tour
'Walkabout' become part of the Queen's repertoire

1969
The tv film Royal Family
The Queen's off-duty life is screened

1972
Royal Tour
The Queen tours South East Asia and the Indian Ocean.
Death of the Duke of Windsor

1973
Britain & Europe
Britain joins the Common market

1977
Queen's Silver Jubilee
Australian and Pacific Tour followed by Canadian
and Caribbean Tour and then a tour of Great Britain

1979
Lord Mountbatten assassinated
The Royal family mourns

1981
Shots fired at the Queen
Spectator at Trooping the Colour fires six blanks shots at the Queen

1981
Prince Charles marries
Marriage of Prince Charles to Lady Diana Spencer in Westminster Abbey

1982
Falklands War
Prince Andrew does operational service

1982
Birth of Prince William
The Royal line is secured for another generation

1984
The IRA threat
IRA attempt to blow up Thatcher cabinet at Brighton

1991
The Gulf War
Operation Desert Storm drives Iraq out of Kuwait

1992
Fortieth Anniversary of the Accession
Elizabeth R screened

1992
Windsor Castle fire
Annus Horriblis speech

1993
The Queen visits Lockerbie
The Queen and the Duke of Edinburgh visit Lockerbie to meet families bereaved in the Pan Am bombing of 1988

1997
Death of Princess Diana
The nation mourns a much loved Princess

1998
Prince Charles 50th
50th birthday of The Queen's eldest son, the Prince of Wales

1999
Royal marriage
The marriage of Prince Edward to Sophie Rhys-Jones takes place at St Georges Chapel, Windsor

2000
Queen Mother's 100th
Queen Elizabeth the Queen Mother celebrates her 100th birthday. The Queen sends her mother her traditional birthday message for centenarians

2002
Queen Mother dies
Queen Elizabeth the Queen Mother dies at 101

2002
The Queen's Golden Jubilee
The nation celebrates the 50th anniversary of the accession to the throne of Queen Elizabeth II

In total, there are 120 coaches in the Royal collection including so-called Sociable carriages as well as several Phaeton carriages which date back to the reign of Queen Victoria. These are used by the Queen from time to time. There are also two Victorias, painted in the maroon royal livery made specifically for Queen Victoria to use in her old age. There are also other examples of various carriages including the Lonsdale Wagonette, the Curricle, the Charabanc, the French Chaise and the Pony Phaeton. Also in the collection are two snow sleighs which Queen Victoria gave to her husband Prince Albert in 1850. Apparently, during one snowy winter Prince Albert too a sleigh to Brighton and rode it near the Royal Pavilion.

The meaning of the word 'Mews' comes from the French word mue which, in turn, is derived from the Latin mutari, to change. This verb refers to changing of skin, coat or feathers. In the Middle Ages a 'mews' was the place where the sovereign's falcons were kept during their 'mewing' – the changing of their plumage.

King Richard 11 (1377-99) was believed to have been the first monarch in Britain to establish a King's Mews, which was located near Charing Cross on the north side of what is now known as Trafalgar Square. Until the reign of King Henry V111 they were used solely for housing falcons.

The Royal Mews was built during the reigns of Edward V1 and Mary 1 but in 1732 King George 11 ordered them to be demolished and new stables built. In 1762 George 111 bought Buckingham House and the Royal Mews was established at the side of the great house. In 1824, George 1V commissioned the famous architect John Nash to redesign the stables and coach houses and they became the Royal Mews in 1825, the date shown on the weathercock above the porch. The Mews consists of a quadrangle approached from Buckingham

Palace Road by a Doric arch surmounted by a clock tower. The east side of the block is occupied by the State coaches and the north and west quarters house the magnificent stables. Behind the quadrangle are more coach houses in which all the Royal cars are garaged. Above these buildings are modernised apartments where the married coachmen, grooms and chauffeurs live.

There is also one horse in the Royal Mews at Buckingham Palace reserved exclusively for Prince Philip, a charger by the name of Philippa, so named because she was born on Prince Philip's birthday and given to him as a present by the Queen. Philip occasionally exercises Philippa in the indoor school and sometimes rides out around the 60 acre garden of Buckingham Palace. He is in fact the only person permitted to do so.

One hundred thousand visitors a year flood into the Royal Mews to view the wonderful array of coaches, carriages, harnesses, the magnificent horses and the memorabilia on display.

For the past seven years Colin Henderson has been the Head Coachman after serving thirty years in the Household Cavalry. He has a team of thirty including restorers, harness makers and seventeen stable staff who groom, ride and care for the horses.

Every Christmas the Queen attends a children's party at the Royal Mews and also tours the Mews, checking all the horses and chatting to the staff. She also casts her eye over the eleven Windsor greys currently stabled there and knows all their names – St. Patrick, King's Troop, Auckland, Jubilee, Britannia, Iceland, Dresden, Alderney, Hillsborough, Windhoek and Twilight. It will only be decided which eight will pull the Coronation Coach to St. Paul's for the Queen's thanksgiving for the Golden Jubilee a few days before the event, depending on the condition and temperament of each horse.

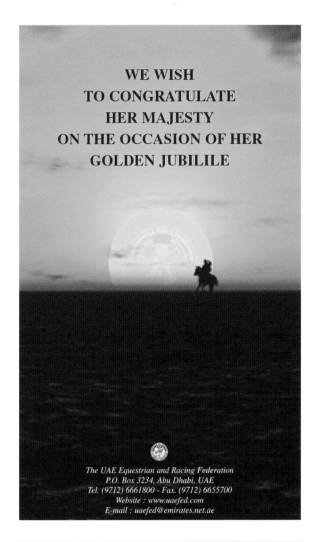

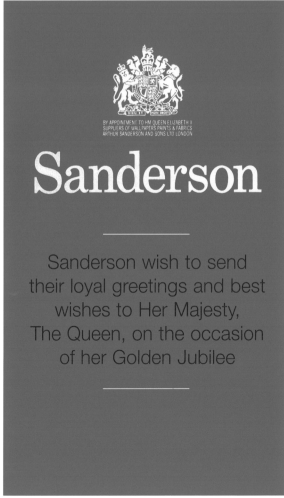

'I'm taking the short route. Hold on!' Lt Col Sir John Miller, the Crown Equerry, Horsemaster to the Queen, suddenly produced a hunting horn from his pocket and blew a series of stirring blasts as he swung his four-in-hand team diagonally downhill. Seated next to him in the dubious role of 'referee', I clutched the side of the wagonette with one hand and rammed down my bowler with the other. Four of the Queen's horses were pulling us downhill at an increasing canter towards the shimmering expanse of Virginia Water. It occurred to me that baling out in the water might be the best option if we were thundering into disaster. That option never occurred. You never foresee the exact nature of a disaster. At the edge of the water the team suddenly swung back up the hill. The wagonette jack-knifed and crashed to its nearside – my side.

Sir John nimbly leapt over me as we hit the ground, never letting go of the reins. I recall a melee of flashing hooves, twisted harness and some splintered wood. Somehow Sir John brought the team to a halt halfway up the hill and his groom was soon holding the horses' heads. It was no surprise to me to find out later that a photographer covering that 1975 International Driving Grand Prix won Sports Picture of the Year Award with his shot of this 'incident'.

Sir John, his navigator, the groom and I survived unhurt. I sprang to my feet all the more quickly when I realised that a lady spectator in sunglasses approaching to enquire after my health was Her Majesty the Queen. Surprise number two was that we were 'going on'. The Queen and everyone else present seemed to accept this as perfectly reasonable, even though one of the wagonette's four wheels was now missing. To my horror a driving enthusiast cut a large branch from a nearby tree,

with immediate royal permission, and this was lashed with rope to an axle. Sir John, without comment or change of expression, then drove his team through Virginia Water, with the wagonette at an alarming angle because it was supported only by the 'skid stick'.

I was not particularly surprised at the next section marked 'gallop' when Sir John duly galloped his three-wheeled contraption. I had lost my referee's clipboard and pencil, but could not have ventured any coherent official comment by then. Soon after the gallop, the wagonette keeled over further and, in passing, struck a gatepost. Its springs gave way, and it subsided quite gently to the ground, without any wheels. Our journey was over. I recall walking through woodland, leading one of the Queen's horses. Her Majesty suddenly appeared in a Land-Rover and calmly enquired: 'Are all my horses safe?' The Virginia Water incident throws light on the characters of all concerned, not least that of Sir John Mansel Miller. His background and career might at first glance seem conventional, but anyone who knows the former Crown Equerry will testify that he is a singular and exceptional personality. It was fortunate that he played such a major role for 26 years in organising the coach and horses element in royal pageantry, viewed by millions all over the world on TV.

The State Opening of Parliament, the annual Queen's Birthday Parade, Royal Ascot and visits by foreign heads of state are regular high points in the Crown Equerry's calendar. He has to ensure that 'all the Queen's horses' from the Royal Mews are ready and able to perform superbly amid the pressures of huge public occasions, including four royal weddings. As well as his official duties Sir John played a crucial role in assisting the Queen and her family to enjoy and expand their horsey interests in an amazingly wide variety of sports, all containing a substantial element of risk: Prince Philip's competition and coach driving; Prince Charles's polo and hunting; and Princess Anne's eventing. Providing and maintaining horses for the Queen to ride out hacking and in public at Trooping the Colour is another major responsibility for the Crown Equerry and his staff.

During his tenure of office and ever since Sir John has advised and assisted the Queen with breeding an extraordinary array of horses and ponies for all of the above sports, as well as for such bizarre projects as endeavouring to breed those huge skewbald drum horses for the Household Cavalry.

John Miller was born on 4 February 1919 into an Oxfordshire military family, being the third son of Brigadier General Alfred Miller who commanded the Royal Scots Greys. John Miller's great-grandfather was MP for Glamorgan for 50 years and Father of the House of Commons. Horses played a major part in John Miller's boyhood at the family home, Shotover House near Oxford, where he still lives. He hunted with the South Oxfordshire, of which his father was Master. After Eton and Sandhurst he was commissioned in 1939 in the Welsh Guards, and his attitude to risk was reflected in his highly distinguished war record. For his part in the fierce fighting in the Northern European campaign after the Allied landings he was awarded the DSO and MC. He was commanding the 1st Battalion Welsh Guards when he was appointed Crown Equerry in 1961. His wide experience as a horseman, especially his interest in breeding top-class animals, soon proved a boon to the royal family. Princess Anne's remarkable eventing career began on Purple Star, one of seven foals born to Sir John's favourite mare Stella. He finished seventh on Stella in Badminton Horse Trials in 1951 and was a candidate for Britain's event team in the Helsinki Olympics in 1952, but a vertebrae broken in a fall robbed him of this chance.

One of the major successes in the Queen's venture of breeding polo ponies for Prince Charles to ride was the use of the small thoroughbred stallion, College Green. Sir John found the stallion living very comfortably in an old railway wagon near Scarborough, the property of a local butcher. Obligingly a small boy jumped on the stallion to ride him bareback round a field for the Crown Equerry to see. Clearly it was an equable animal and Sir John purchased it for £250 in 1968, one of many economical deals he carried out for his royal employers.

One of the foundation mares used by the Queen was Suerte from the Argentine. Her foal, by the stallion Doubtless II, was intended for the polo field, but grew too big at 16.2 hands. This was immensely fortunate for Princess Anne who was given the foal, a chestnut gelding named Doublet. He was a tremendous success in the demanding sport of eventing, and was her partner in her biggest triumph – winning the individual European Three Day Event Championship at Burghley in 1971.

Sir John enthusiastically embraced the hazardous and exciting sport of combined carriage driving, including a marathon phase involving daunting obstacles across country, when it was born in the early 1970s. Prince Philip took up the sport in 1973, using five bays from the Royal Mews, and became its leader and inspiration. There was a breeding element in the driving venture too. Sir John judiciously mixed Oldenburg blood with some of the traditional Cleveland bays in the royal stables to produce horses that could perform faster across country in competition, but could still appear successfully on ceremonial occasions. Some of the royal breeding projects take place at the royal stud at Hampton Court, which Sir John continued to oversee in retirement.

After the Prince of Wales thoroughly enjoyed his very first day's fox-hunting with the Beaufort Hunt in February 1975, Sir John Miller found suitable horses and made arrangements for the Prince to explore the hunting field all over Britain. He accompanied Prince Charles on visits to over 40 different hunts, which involved riding a huge variety of terrains and obstacles ranging from fly fences to timber and stone walls, or miles of open moorland. It was to be a remarkable way of exploring rural Britain on horseback. The Prince met professional huntsmen and many farmers who have remained his friends ever since, visiting him regularly at Highgrove.

As well as all the pressures of supervising the royal equestrian and motor transport from the Royal Mews, Sir John has maintained a much wider role in the equestrian world. He ensured that the Royal Mews survived as a centre of equestrian life in London. School children, children with disabilities and riding club members ride regularly in the indoor riding school at the Mews, and many horse societies and equine charities hold meetings there.

Knighted in 1974, Sir John Miller was appointed a Knight Grand Cross of the Victorian order in 1987. His immense contribution to 'all the Queen's horses' is not widely known to the general public, but the legacy of his work is profoundly demonstrated by the prime place of the horse in our celebration of Her Majesty's Golden Jubilee.

**LAND ROVER THE WORLD OVER
CONGRATULATES HER MAJESTY QUEEN ELIZABETH II
ON HER GOLDEN JUBILEE.**

THE LAND ROVER EXPERIENCE

Polo, Eventing and Carriage Driving

Throughout her life the Queen has enjoyed a close relationship with the game of polo. Many have suggested that though horse racing is the sport of kings, polo is the sport of princes. It is certainly true of the British Royal family for the Queen's great enthusiasm and interest in horse racing is matched by the interest Prince Philip and Prince Charles have shown in playing polo which has now been taken up most energetically by her grandsons, Prince William and Prince Harry. And though the Queen has never been known to actually play in a polo match she has supported the sport by breeding polo ponies and has, on occasion, presented both Prince Philip and Prince Charles with ponies that she had believed would be suitable for them and for their polo.

Her interest in the game began in Malta, the Mediterranean island where both Prince Philip and his uncle, Earl Mountbatten were stationed with the Royal Navy after the second World War. In those early years of her marriage, the then Princess Elizabeth was an officer's wife on Malta and was always a keen spectator at the weekly polo matches in which Prince Philip and Earl Mountbatten would be playing for the Royal navy team. And, of course, she would often be asked to present the cups and trophies after the matches. Her interest continued after the war and the Queen readily gave permission for a Guards Polo Club to be granted the use of several polo pitches within Windsor Great Park and establish the club's headquarters there. And, ever since, the Queen has spent many a summer's Sunday afternoon watching polo matches in which, of course, she would frequently have a close family interest.

As a result, the Queen decided to study the breeding of polo ponies to see if it was possible to improve on the varied and many attributes required to make a high goal polo pony. Polo had undergone many changes since it was first brought to Britain from India at the end of the nineteenth century and the game became much faster and more exciting which put greater demands on the ponies. For many years after the second World War the great majority of high-goal ponies were imported from Argentina where for decades the ponies had been schooled to round-up cattle, learning skills which made them near perfect polo ponies; calm and courageous, and capable of sharp turns, quick acceleration and with great brakes. But during the past forty years polo has become even faster and the demands on the ponies greater. Speed became ever more essential in a high-goal polo pony and many ponies were sired by former flat race stallions.

As a result of the Queen's natural instinct and understanding of breeding ponies and horses, a number of polo ponies were bred at the Royal Windsor stud which the Queen has then presented to either Prince Philip or Prince Charles – and nearly all these ponies have gone on to play high-goal polo. Major Ronald Ferguson played alongside Prince Philip in many polo teams and he believes that the enthusiasm and determination of Prince Philip was responsible to a great degree for the Guards Polo Club being given permission to play on Smith's Lawn, Windsor Great Park. As a result, the enthusiasm for polo took off and the single most important international polo match of the year – against America, Argentine or France in particular – grew dramatically and in the 1980s attracted tens of thousands of spectators.

Major Ferguson was later to become Polo Manager to Prince Charles and for twenty-one years was responsible for organising Charles's games and matches so that they didn't clash with his royal duties. It was a formidable task.

Opposite and above:
The Queen at Smiths Lawn, Windsor Great Park where she regularly watches polo matches

Above: Prince Harry with his father the Prince of Wales on the polo field at Cirencester Park, Gloucestershire

Major Ferguson has firm views on the two princes abilities, "Prince Philip was always a very strong, aggressive player and became a first class polo player, keen to win at all costs and very, very difficult to knock off the ball."

"It seemed to me that Prince Philip needed to play polo to get rid of all his pent-up frustrations. He would arrive to play a few chukkas with steam coming out of his ears and after a few games he would be a different man – the frustration gone. Prince Charles on the other hand was not so aggressive as his father but was probably the more skilful player. He relied less on strength and aggression and more on skill and tactics. However, Charles could not afford as much time as was necessary to make him into a great player. Charles was greatly encouraged by Lord Mountbatten who would cheer him on from the sidelines, offering advice and urging him on. However, it was the Australian high-goal player Sinclair Hill who was responsible for Charles's training during his early playing years. Charles had great respect for him. He was tough on Charles but always fair and Charles liked that. At first, of course, Charles relied on his father's cast-off ponies but later the Queen bred ponies for him and presented him with others she thought might be more suitable to polo than any other equestrian discipline."

"Both Prince Charles and his father were passionate about the sport though neither were natural horsemen. Charles was probably the better horseman because, as well as playing polo Charles hunted regularly in the winter and enjoyed team racing whereas Prince Philip was almost exclusively a polo player, enjoying the occasional hack."

The Queen has been an enthusiastic horsewoman from her earliest days when she would ride out with her sister, Princess Margaret, sometimes accompanied by their beloved father. Their ponies were kept in the Royal Family's private stables at Windsor. Most of these ponies and horses were treated more like pets than working horses. The ponies were always confident and friendly, nosing up to visitors looking for the odd carrot, apple or polo mint or nuzzling into people who stroked and patted them. Betsy, a dark brown mare with a blaze down the centre of her face was Elizabeth's favourite in her teenage years; a good-looking 15 hand horse with a sensitive mouth, good manners and a happy and serene temperament. There would be many others that the Queen would favour, some hacks staying at Windsor, others at Balmoral. Riding has always been the Queen's favourite pastime and, today, she still loves to relax at weekends and enjoy a good hour's horse ride, walking, trotting and cantering across the open spaces of Windsor Great Park or the countryside around Balmoral. The Queen passed on her enthusiasm for horse riding to her daughter Princess Anne who combined the positive style of father with the riding skills of her mother. As a result, Princess Anne would become a first class horse-woman, reaching the pinnacle of the sport by being chosen to represent Britain in the Montreal Olympics of 1976.

In 1968, Princess Anne made the momentous decision to concentrate on the toughest equestrian sport – eventing. She had been encouraged by her mother and by the former Crown Equerry, Sir John Miller, himself a brilliant rider and a former member of the British three-day event team. She was fortunate that the independent minded Mrs. Alison Oliver, one of Britain's best event coaches, agreed to become her trainer.

Anne was fortunate in having three first class horses, Purple Star, owned by Sir John Miller, Doublet, which had been a present from the Queen and Royal Ocean, a 16.2 hands Irish thoroughbred. From 1968 riding became almost a full-time occupation for the young princess and, remarkably, three years later she was selected to ride in the world three day event at Badminton which attracted riders from the USA, Canada, Australia and Europe. Many believed the Princess was being over ambitious but she confounded the critics and, riding Doublet, and watched by members of the Royal Family she finished fifth – an amazing performance from someone who had only recently entered senior competitions.

Months later at Burghley House in Lincolnshire, Princess Anne amazed the horse world once more by winning the European Three Day Event in great style. And once again she had been riding the Queen's little chestnut gelding Doublet. Indeed, the measure of her success was illustrated because Princess Anne and Doublet had beaten the reigning world champion, the current winner of Badminton and an Olympic gold medallist. In 1974 however,

Doublet broke a leg while Princess Anne was riding him in Windsor Great Park and had to be put down. In tears, an inconsolable Princess Anne commented later, "It was the most ghastly experience of my entire life."

But Princess Anne was selected as a member of the British Olympic team for the Montreal games in 1976 riding Goodwill, a 16.2 hands brown gelding bought by the Queen for her daughter on the advice of Alison Oliver. Anne and Goodwill became a formidable team but those Olympic games proved to be a true test of Anne's courage, determination and stamina. And though she took a hard spectacular fall which knocked her unconscious, she insisted on continuing and ended 24th, a great achievement. Anne continued to ride in top-grade competitions but never again made the Olympic team though she had many successes in the toughest of horse trials.

Prince Philip decided to take up the sport of carriage driving when he had to give up polo because of arthritis affecting his right hand which made it all but impossible to grip the polo stick. Aggressive and adventurous, Prince Philip took to carriage driving with great enthusiasm and remarkable success. He enjoyed the competitive nature of the sport and the challenge of having to cope with a team of horses. Indeed, carriage driving became far and away his favourite hobby. During the past few years carriage driving has become the fastest growing equitation sport in the country and many young people have now discovered the challenge and the thrills and spills of the sport.

Above: Queen Elizabeth at the Coronation Cup presentations with a dejected looking England team, who lost 10-9 in extra time to Argentina, at the Cartier International 2000 Polo at Windsor

At first, Prince Philip used the Royal bays stabled at the Royal Mews but some ten years ago he switched to driving a team of four Fell ponies from the Queen's Balmoral estate. For more than twenty years Prince Philip has toured the country taking part in National driving events and competitions held at weekends in many stately homes around Britain. He competes in not only team driving but also singles, pairs and tandem driving often watched by the Queen, especially when Prince Philip is competing at the Windsor Horse Trials. Team driving is the pinnacle of this exciting sport and Prince Philip became so proficient that he not only represented Britain but also won a gold medal.

Carriage driving is not a sport for the faint-hearted or those not strong and tough enough to compete in the marathon events which usually take some one-and-a-half hours to complete. These events include two ten kilometre trotting sections and two five kilometre walks, and finish with a dramatic six to eight kilometre cross-country section with eight obstacles and against the clock. Drivers can gallop as fast as they want on this last section and many need to do so just to remain within the time limit. It is during this discipline that many of the spills occur and Prince Philip has enjoyed his share of tumbles.

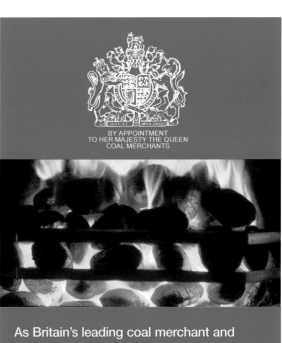

Catherston Stud wishes to congratulate Her Majesty Queen Elizabeth 11 on the occasion of her Golden Jubilee

The Loriston-Clarke family is proud to be associated with All the Queen's Horses. Catherston Stud was founded over 50 years ago and has been breeding and training horses and ponies for all disciplines from Pony Club to Olympic level ever since. The breeding dynasty founded by Dutch Courage, Jennie's World Dressage Bronze Medal Ride, is going from strength to strength and from his sons are being bred the International competition horses of today and tomorrow.

For further information contact : Catherston Stud Croft Farm, Over Wallop, Stockbridge, Hants SO20 8HX. Tel +44 (01264) 782716 Fax +44 (01264) 782717. E-mail catherston.stud@ukgateway.net

Royal Windsor Horse Show

There is no more appropriate place to pay an equestrian tribute to The Queen than the Royal Windsor Horse Show. It is an event that has been closely associated with the Monarch and other Members of the Royal Family since 1943.

Few sights can compare to that on the Sunday night of Royal Windsor Horse Show, when a spectacular firework display lights up the sky above the picturesque town of Windsor, with the stunning backdrop of a floodlit Windsor Castle. For splendour, tradition and fun, Royal Windsor Horse Show is unrivalled. Royal Windsor Horse Show began life as a "horse show, gymkhana and dog show" in the then King, George VI's back garden, Home Park, Windsor. It was the idea of Geoffrey Cross, a bombadier recently invalided from the Army and keen to do something for the war effort. Along with his close friend, Count Robert Orssich, he organised a horse show during "Wings for Victory" week in November 1943.

Permission was granted from the King to hold it at Windsor Castle and so an event was born that has grown in prestige and standing to make it a highlight of the equestrian, social and royal calendar that it is today. In 1943 however, it was such a low-key event that the results weren't worthy of a mention in Horse & Hound, The Royal Family sat in garden chairs under an awning, and a stray lurcher stole a chicken from the catering tent and ate it under the King's chair.

The dog show at Royal Windsor was short-lived as the 1943 show turned out not to have conformed with any Kennel Club Rules and Geoffrey Cross vowed there would be no more dogs. The show did however raise £1,500 for

"Wings for Victory" and spawned the Royal Windsor Show Club. King George VI became its first Patron.

In 1944, it was not so much the competitions that drew the crowds as the competitors. Almost 8,000 spectators turned out to watch the mixture of showing, hunter and driving classes. In particular they were treated to watching the then Princess Elizabeth and her sister Princess Margaret taking part in the Single Pony Private Driving. The following year The Princesses won the Turn Out Class with a Norwegian pony called Hans that belonged to the King and from this moment on Royal Family participation became as much a trademark of the Show as its glorious setting.

Carriage Driving Trials were introduced to Royal Windsor in the 70's and Prince Philip, later to be a member of the British team at the World Driving Championships was its most famous competitor. In 1976 a broken carriage trace in the last phase of the International Driving Grand Prix cost him victory. He is still a regular competitor in the Driving Classes with his team of Fells, owned by HM The Queen.

Princess Anne also joined the ranks of Royals actively participating at "their show". She took part in the combined training during the 70's with various horses, winning it with Doublet who later went on carry her to an individual Gold Medal in the 1973 European Three Day Event Championships.

The Military plays a great part in Royal Windsor and in particular The Household Cavalry and The King's Troop. Visiting displays from abroad have included the Royal Canadian Mounted Police whose musical ride dates back from 1876 and whose first performance at Windsor was in 1957. In the early years of the Show the Services Team Jumping was one of the major attractions and is still a fiercely fought-out jumping competition between all services. In 2002 the Skill at Arms, another inter-regimental competition has attracted entries from as far afield as the United States. The Prince of Wales, in his position of Colonel of the Welsh Guards, took part in the Services Triathlon in 1979 and finished third.

The Show today takes over 3,000 entries for its variety of classes, pays out £70,000 in prize money and attracts around 60,000 visitors over the five days. It is not purely for the equestrian enthusiast. The appeal is still in the "great day out for all the family" aspect. Hundreds of trade stands provide shopping to cater for everyone, whether you are looking for designer labels, pet care goods, cars or walking shoes.

Above: The Duke of Edinburgh at the Royal Windsor Horse Show

Right: International show jumper, Nigel Coupe at the Royal Windsor Horse Show, 1996

Opposite top: Youngsters taking part in The Shetland Pony Grand National at The Royal Windsor Horse Show

Bottom: Participants in the carriage driving competition setting out along the Royal Mile in front of Windsor Castle

The main attraction in the Castle Arena this year will be the Tandem display by La Garde Republicaine, the French Presidential Guard, along with top class show jumping and old favourites like the Shetland Pony Grand National.

At this Royal Windsor Horse Show the Queen will take the salute for her Jubilee Tribute – "All The Queen's Horses"- on Saturday night. Other Royal visitors will include HRH The Princess Royal and HRH the Earl of Wessex

All The Queen's Horses takes place on Thursday, Friday and Saturday evenings. Her Majesty's lifetime love of horses and especially racing will be reflected in the ninety-minute equestrian stage show which fits naturally into the setting of Royal Windsor.

Geoffrey Cross can hardly have imagined, in 1943, how his charity "gymkhana" would grow to become the most royal of Royal Shows. Its place in history and in the history of Windsor and the Royal Family is now irrevocably established and in 2002 Royal Windsor Horse Show and All The Queen's Horses will provide one of the most spectacular equestrian theatrical displays ever staged.

Official Merchandise

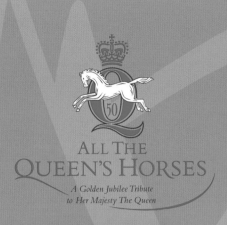

ALL THE QUEEN'S HORSES
A Golden Jubilee Tribute to Her Majesty The Queen

T&G Long sleeve drill shirt	Regatta blue	M, L, XL	£ 49.95
Short sleeve drill shirt	Regatta blue	M, L, XL	£ 46.50
Long sleeve kid's drill shirt	Regatta blue	M, L, XL	£ 29.95
T-shirt with pocket	White	M, L, XL	£ 19.95
Polo Shirt	Regatta blue	M, L, XL	£ 34.95
Caps	Light blue	one size	
	Regatta blue	one size	£ 16.50
Kid's caps	Regatta blue	one size	£ 13.50
T&G Waterproof jacket	Regatta blue	M, L, XL	£115.00

To place an order please visit our website at:

www.tandg.co.uk

Or 'phone us on:

01264 811000

Or visit us at stand numbers M1 and W1, The Royal Windsor Horse Show, Home Park, Windsor, on the 15th, 16th, 17th, 18th and 19th of May 2002.

Above: Water obstacles pose a substantial challenge to carriage driving teams. This dramatic photograph illustrates the degree of difficulty.

Left and below: Scenes from past carriage driving competitions. The Duke of Edinburgh has been a competitor for many years.

Above and below: Scenes from recent Royal Windsor Horse Shows. The weather has varied over the years, but the only time it has been cancelled was due to the Foot and Mouth epidemic in 2001.

Centre picture: The panorama shows The Royal Windsor Horse Show show - ground as seen from Windsor Castle.

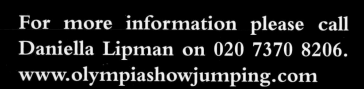

Balmoral

The wild and beautiful 50,000 acre estate of Balmoral Castle in Aberdeenshire, Scotland, is the Queen's favourite home where she spends her summer holidays and the New Year. A private estate, owned by the Queen personally, Balmoral is where she loves to relax, walk in the fresh mountain air, stalk deer and to ride. The extensive moorland and mountain estate lies on either side of the road from Ballater, past the tiny village of Balmoral, towards Braemar, and then over the pass of the Devil's Elbow towards the south. Visitors pass through the hamlet of Crathie, past the tiny church away on the right where the Royal Family worship, and see before them Balmoral Castle nestled in the foreground of a range of conical hills.

Behind the castle, the lower slopes of the hills are fir-clad, brown and dun with occasional rocky outcrops and, at the top, sparsely covered with tiny arctic birch trees. In autumn, the hills which rise from the Castle in every direction, are dense with heather providing a fairy-tale setting. And standing amidst this wild splendour is the solitary granite castle. As far as the eye can see are tens of thousands of pine providing not only pricavy but sensational riding. The hills close to the Castle include two of the home beats where small herds of deer may be seen as they graze. Further afield are some of the other famous beats such as Abergeldie, Bachnagin, Gelder and the Spittal where throughout her reign the Queen has enjoyed days of long, gruelling stalking and miles of punishing walking sometimes climbing to more than 2,000 feet. And below these hills, winding through the estate, can be seen the River Dee, the clear, sparkling water meandering slowly down stream in the summer months but rushing in foaming torrents after heavy rains.

Most days when the Queen is in residence she loves to hack out, usually with one of her favourite gillies but sometimes with a member of the family.

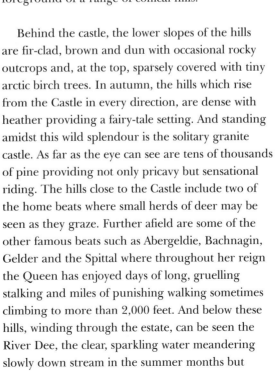

But Balmoral is primarily enjoyed by the Queen for her favourite sport of deer stalking and it is, of course, why Balmoral is famous for its deer ponies, the Garrons and the Fells, renowned for being hardy, tough and wiry. Some of the Queen's Fell ponies were foaled at Windsor and sent to Scotland while others were bred at Balmoral. Sturdy and powerful, the black-coated Fells make wonderful driving ponies. They are also used for work at Balmoral but for muscular strength and sturdiness, endurance and surefootedness the garrons are without rivals. These ponies can climb hills all day, keep their balance on the steepest, most difficult terrain and carry home a fifteen stone stag on their backs.

One of the Queen's favourites, a Garron nicknamed 'The Tank' was so-called because he could cover the roughest ground at great speed and carry the dead-weight of the heaviest stag ten miles or more without a stop. But these rough-coated deer ponies are not mollycoddled or pampered; they live rough no matter how harsh the weather or cold the winter. It is their nature to do so, appearing impervious to cold or rain.

At Balmoral, a large shed is in their paddock but they rarely, if ever, make use of it, not even in winter. A long manger is provided in the shed where, in the hardest winters, corn and hay are supplied but more often that not, the Garrons prefer to stand out in the deepest snow and somehow find sufficient grazing on almost barren pastures.

The Balmoral Garrons are well bred and to ensure the strain remains pure on some occasions a mare is mated with a thoroughbred. And the foaling too is as hardy as their life, the Garron mares happily foaling in the open field. And they live long lives, happily working away for twenty years or more.

The Queen was only sixteen years old when she began to learn the art of deer stalking and it has been one of her great joys ever since. She finds the pastime not only fascinating and interesting but wonderfully relaxing and invigorating. During the eight week season, Balmoral's head stalker will discuss with Prince Philip each morning the best expedition for that day taking into consideration

Above: Her Majesty Queen Elizabeth II fondly stroking her favourite horse 'Betsy' during a visit to Sandringham, January 1964

the deer herds, the weather and the all-important wind direction. But after taking advice the final choice is made by the Queen herself who decides in which direction the Royal party and guests will go.

For much of her reign there have been eight deer ponies at Balmoral and these are divided into pairs before the Queen arrives in late summer. They are then taken off by a gillie and dispersed to the various beats where they remain for the season living off the land. When the Queen stalks a distant beat she would sometimes ride out on one of the ponies near the castle. In recent years, the Queen takes a Range Rover ride as far as possible and will then, if necessary, take a pony ride or simply begin the stalk from that point. Accompanied by the head

stalker the Queen, followed by her guests, will then move forward and upward, passing through the undergrowth, skirting the open spaces and moving from cover to cover, always with the breeze in their faces. The stalking may go from ten in the morning until six or seven in the evening with no rests save for a sandwich lunch. A few hundred yards behind the stalking party the gillies lead the ponies ready to come up after the shot has been fired to carry the heavy deer back to the castle. The Queen, who learned to shoot with a rifle in her teens and rarely uses a shotgun, is described as a 'dead shot'.

It is at this point that the ponies sometimes become nervous for they don't seem to like the idea of the deer, particularly stags, being lifted onto their

A Horse Show
For Everyone!

La Garde Républicaine
British Isles Showing Championship
Show Jumping
Dressage

Military Displays
Town & Country Shopping
Victorian Fun Fair
Sunday Fireworks Spectacular

Discounts on all Advance Bookings
2 FREE child tickets (5 - 15yrs) per adult for Wed, Thurs, and Fri. only
Special rates for advance family bookings (2 adults and 2 children
- Sat. and Sun. only)

Ticket Hotline: 0870 121 5370
15-19 May 2002, Home Park, Windsor Castle
www.royal-windsor-horse-show.co.uk

Royal Windsor
Horse Show

See and Hear The World's Most Famous Horse Whisperer, Monty Roberts
Only on Wednesday 15th, Thursday 16th and Friday 17th. **Book now on 0870 121 5370**

The Queen at Balmoral
Lower left: with Prince Andrew

backs. The gillies overcome the nervousness by placing their coats over the pony's head. However, as soon as the deer has been placed across their backs the ponies don't seem to mind one jot and happily begin the long trek back.

Then the deer ponies come into their own, carrying the dead deer down the mountain to the castle, a distance of sometimes more then ten miles. When their hard day is over the ponies will return to their stables on their beat and the following morning are once again fresh, strong and keen to go.

These ponies have often been likened to Old English sheep dogs with their dishevelled, windswept manes covering their eyes and their rough winter coats. They usually winter in a pasture close to the castle where the head stalker can keep a close eye on them. Indeed, because the ponies live such long lives the relationship between the groom and the ponies seems more like that between a man and his dog. There seems to be an understanding, a kinship.

Put
momentum
into your
PR Strategy

momentu**momentum**omentu
public relations

RUSHMANS

Innovative Sources

of

REVENUE

for

INTERNATIONAL

EVENTS

Accreditation & Media Management

We offer our very best wishes
to Her Majesty The Queen on the
occasion of her Golden Jubilee.
We are proud to have been
associated with this magnificent
tribute, and offer our thanks
and congratulations to
'All The Queen's Horses' chairman
Col. Sir Piers Bengough KCVO OBE,
committee members,
Simon Brooks-Ward and his
team at HorsePower.

www.rushmans.com

Rushmans Limited
1 Lower Grosvenor Place
London SW1W 0EJ
Telephone: 07000 350 000
Fax: 07000 350 111

Horses at Rest

On a flat, vast open plain in the heart of Leicestershire, where winter winds blow hard and chill, lies the nerve-centre of Britain's military animal welfare establishment: the Defence Animal Centre. This historic place has been home to thousands of the Queen's horses during her reign, but during the past two years a modern new camp with all the necessary facilities – has been built close by the historic Victorian buildings that first housed the Royal Army Veterinary Corps at the end of the Second World War.

Today, not only the Royal Army Veterinary Corps, with its state-of-the-art hospital and treatment centre, but also the Army's School of Equitation, the Remount Division and the Canine Division all share the new facilities at the revamped Defence Animal Centre a few miles outside Melton Mowbray. All the horses that are either sent to the Centre or stabled there on a permanent basis are under the command of Her Majesty. The horses – blacks or bays around 16 hands or more – are being evaluated, broken or schooled, enjoying a rest from duties or undergoing treatment or surgery. The Centre's permanently resident horses are used in the School of Equitation for training officers and men of the Household Cavalry and the King's Troop Royal Artillery to the exacting high standards demanded.

Each year, the Commandant of the Defence Animal Centre, the Officer Commanding the Equine Division, the Riding-Master of the Household Cavalry, the Equitation Instructor of the King's Troop and the Centre's Veterinary Surgeon visit southern Ireland in the spring on a buying expedition. A few weeks before flying out, the Commandant contacts a number of horse dealers who have provided good reliable animals in the

past, and asks them to search around for 50 or so suitable horses. The requirements never vary. The Army is looking for good bays or black horses, between three and five years old, between 16 and 16.3 hands tall, sound and in good condition. And the Army wants the majority of them unbroken.

Having been trucked to Melton Mowbray in June, the horses are put into an isolation field for six weeks just in case any of them have any contagious disease that wasn't detected during their initial examination. It is, in fact, quite rare to find that any of them have a disease. They are then inoculated against flu and tetanus, and issued with a 'passport' – the B270 – in which every detail of a horse's life will be entered. After that, the horse is taken to the farrier and given a four-figure Army number, which is branded on to their front hoofs – one number on one foot, three on the other.

After that burst of activity, all the horses are put back into the fields to enjoy the rest of the summer, and come into their stables in the autumn to start their education. The school's celebrated remount riders then take over responsibility for breaking and schooling the new intake of horses so that they will end up well prepared for their ceremonial duties, most of which will be experienced in the heart of London. These young horses, who have known nothing but the peace and quiet of rural life, will have to learn to cope with the noise, the bustle, the vehicles, the spectators, the buildings, the martial music and the discipline of ceremonial life. Sometimes, horses are returned from the Household Cavalry and the King's Troop, not because they are undisciplined, but because they have been unable to settle in to ceremonial life. These horses are re-evaluated and often found suitable for the School of Equitation at Melton

Mowbray. Others are passed on to Military Saddle
Clubs around the country, because these clubs
provide a chance for families of men and women in
the Armed Forces to enjoy riding.

One of the most important features of the Centre
is the 'R and R' (rest and recuperation) it provides
for the Queen's ceremonial horses. The Centre
boasts 365 acres of lovely, good-quality
Leicestershire pasture where, at least once a year,
horses of the Household Cavalry and the King's
Troop can stay for six weeks at a time, a welcome
break from the rigours of ceremonial life. Cavalry
horses tend to make two visits a year while King's
Troop horses have only one visit.

Whilst some military animals rest and some
retire at Melton Mowbray, there is another special
place where old war horses retire. Nestling on the
southern side of the Chilterns, surrounded by
lush, green rolling hills and a smattering of trees
and woods, a hundred or so horses graze peacefully
in the autumn sunshine. They are relaxing and
enjoying their retirement after a life of hard
work – and sometimes danger.

This is Speen Farm in Lacey Green,
Buckinghamshire, the Home of Rest for Horses,
many of which have been owned by the Queen.
A number have spent most of their working lives
in the Royal Mews at Buckingham Palace or seen
service with the Household Cavalry. Some of these
horses have pulled state coaches or carriages on
ceremonial occasions, or pulled the open carriages
in the famous drive down the racecourse each day
the Queen attends Royal Ascot. There are others,
too; a number are former police horses, a few have
been eventers or racehorses and a smattering are
those whose loving owners have simply not wanted
to have their favourite horse put down.

Among the 125 horses fortunate enough to be
retired and living at Speen Farm at the moment are
some that have been seen and admired by hundreds
of thousands of people throughout their lifetime's
work, while there are others who are enjoying a
peaceful life after being seriously injured in
accidents or terrorist bombings. Perhaps the most
famous resident of Speen is the magnificent Janus,
a former drum horse of the Blues and Royals,
who is one of the Queen's favourites. Now aged
18 and standing some 17.3 hands, the huge

Dodson & Horrell
congratulate Her Majesty
on her Golden Jubilee

Dodson & Horrell Ltd - honoured to be providing top
quality horse feed to the Household Cavalry and Kings Troop
Royal Horse Artillery for nearly 20 years

DODSON & HORRELL
LIMITED
Feed Specialists

Dodson & Horrell Limited, Ringstead, Kettering, Northants NN14 4BX Tel: +44(0)1832 737300 Fax: +44(0)1832 737303
E-mail: enquiries@dodsonandhorrell.com www.dodsonandhorrell.com

skewbald weighs more than a ton! Yet Janus is a gentle giant. Brigadier Paul Jepson, Chief Executive and Veterinary Director of Speen Farm and the Queen's Honorary Veterinary Surgeon, recalls one day in 1996 when the Queen visited the Army School of Equitation at Melton Mowbray, which is also the Household Cavalry's Remount Centre. 'The Queen was walking around the school, looking at all the horses when she saw Janus standing at the back of a group. She recognised him instantly, patted him and talked to him like an old friend. In that moment I realised how close the Queen is to many of her horses. She really has a deep affection for them.'

And then there is the veteran of the home, the courageous Echo, a 16.1-hand grey who was

seriously injured when the IRA set off a huge bomb at Hyde Park Corner in July 1982 as 16 men of the Life Guards, escorted by police, rode out of Knightsbridge Barracks for the Changing of the Guard ceremony. In that horrific bombing, the IRA killed 8 soldiers, injured 51 other people and, in the carnage, 10 horses had to be destroyed and several others were injured by flying metal. After the bombing, Echo – one of the Metropolitan police horses that day – became a nervous wreck, unable to be tacked up or to accept any rider who tried to mount him. He was even nervous in his box, constantly trembling and getting colic whenever a stranger approached.

Vets agreed that Echo would never recover fully and so he was sent to Speen. Even in the tranquillity

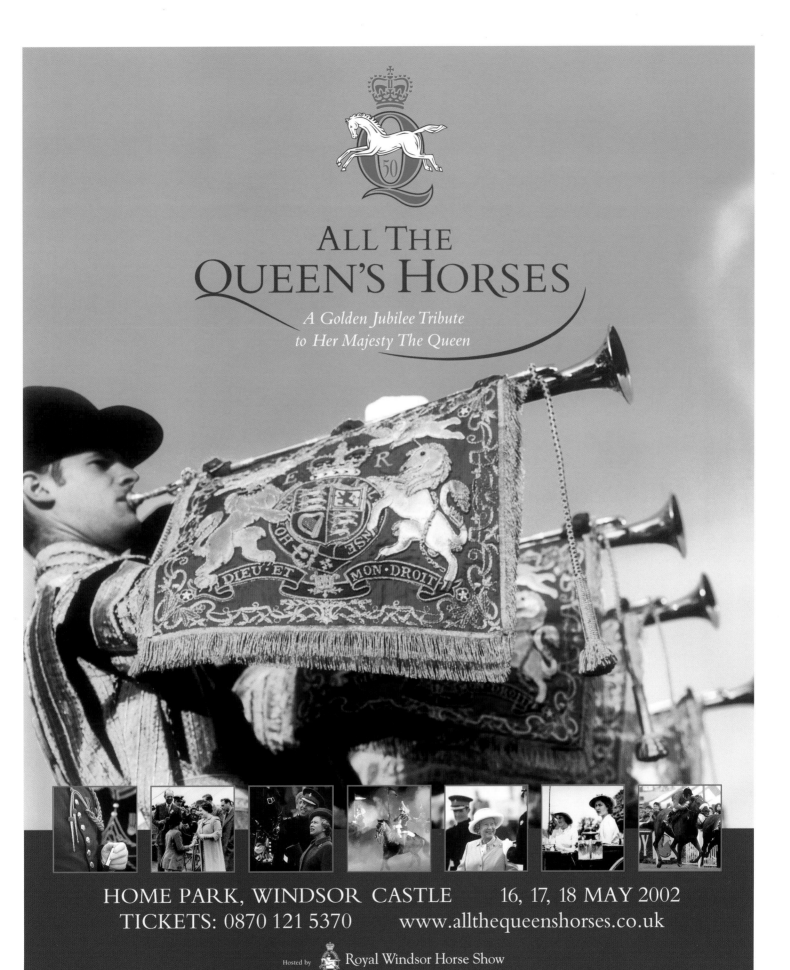

of the countryside, it took Echo a couple of years to relax totally and now he is more like a pet dog than a horse. He follows his groom around, walks to heel and is perfectly behaved. His fear of strangers has also disappeared and, at the age of 30, he is now enjoying a peaceful life. But he has never forgotten the trauma of the IRA bomb and today – 20 years later – cannot be boxed, becoming panicky whenever grooms have tried to put him in a horse box.

Starlight, a beautiful grey Hanoverian – one of the Queen's horses that lived in the Royal Mews and pulled the royal coaches – was retired to Speen in 1997 after a lifetime of royal service. He pulled the grandest state coaches on royal ceremonial occasions

for some ten years but suffered from navicular – a disease of the hoof – and, as a result, had to be retired.

The foundation of the Home of Rest for Horses was largely due to the efforts of one woman, Miss Ann Lindo, who was appalled at the treatment of many of the working horses on London's streets. In May 1886 it was agreed that a home of rest for horses, mules and donkeys should be opened, and balls and dinners were organised to raise funds.

HRH Prince Albert pledged his support and the Duke of Portland, Master of the Royal Household, became President. A farm at Sudbury, near Harrow,